THE VITAL
CHURCH LEADER

EFFECTIVE CHURCH SERIES

R. ROBERT CUENI
Edited by HERB MILLER

THE VITAL CHURCH LEADER

ABINGDON PRESS

Nashville

The Vital Church Leader

Copyright © 1991 by Abingdon Press

This book is printed on acid-free paper.

Library of Congress Cataloging-in-Publication Data

CUENI, R. ROBERT.
   The vital church leader / R. Robert Cueni.
   p. cm. — (The effective church series)
   Includes bibliographical references.
   ISBN 0-687-43793-8 (alk. paper)
   1. Christian leadership. 2. Clergy—Office. I. Title. II. Series.
BV652.1.C84   1990
253—dc20
                                        90-44549
                                            CIP

Manufactured in the United States of America

To Karen and Colleen, my beloved daughters

CONTENTS

THE VITAL
CHURCH LEADER

FOREWORD

"Why?" is the most important question that church leaders can ask: "Why should we do this particular ministry task?" Failure to answer that question in a valid, biblical way wastes tons of leadership energy. Programmatic ships that should never have been built sail out of the harbor for meaningless cruises.

After we ask why, inevitably we ask how: "How should we do this particular ministry task?" A young board chairman sat down in his pastor's office with a cup of coffee in hand. Upon the recommendation of a special task force, the board had made an important decision the preceding evening that had turned the church in a new direction. "I think our people want to be more effective in what the task force wants us to do," he said. "I just don't think they know how." Some form of that conversation happens in countless congregations every day. "Why?" is the most important question, but "how?" is the most frequently asked—and far more difficult—question to answer. Deftly deflecting a how question with "How do *you* think we should do it?" is a good counseling technique but not sufficient. Laypersons want and expect straight, helpful answers to their "how to do it" inquiries. If they do not get those answers, church work begun with high motivation and unselfishly donated time shipwrecks on the rocks of insufficient information. Each volume of the Effective Church Series will help meet the need for "how to" answers in a specific area of church life. These books will provide clergy and laypersons with practical insights and methods that can increase their congregation's effectiveness in achieving God's purposes in every aspect of ministry: leadership, worship, Sunday school, membership care, biblical literacy, spiritual growth, small groups, evangelism, new member assimilation, prayer, youth work, singles work, young adult work, time management, stewardship, administration, community service, world mission, conflict resolution, writing skills.

This first volume stakes out the boundaries of the territory on which other books in the Effective Church Series will build. The vision of vital congregations and the need for more churches to live up to that term is washing across the beaches of all denominations. Yet, no one has told us exactly how to do that. By asking and answering diagnostic questions in ten areas of ministry, that are crucial to congregational vitality, this book does that. Readers and church groups can analyze and plan by looking at their congregation's image, which is reflected in the mirror of these questions.

Philosopher Alfred North Whitehead once advised a science student to seek simplicity and distrust it. Too few church leaders have heeded that counsel. The answer to "how" questions in larger, metropolitan churches is often quite different from the answer in a small rural church. Therefore, each volume in the Effective Church Series will take special care to illustrate the differences in how a method applies to congregations of different sizes and settings.

An insurance salesman stuck his head into a department store sales manager's office door and said, "You don't want to buy any insurance, do you?"

"Young man, who taught you how to sell? Don't ever ask that kind of question!" After a long lecture on salesmanship, in which he stressed that every customer's needs are different, the sales manager said, "Your problem is a lack of confidence. Give me an application blank. I'll buy some insurance from you to give you confidence in yourself." After completing the application, the sales manager gave the young salesman his closing lecture: "Now remember what I told you. Each customer is different. Figure out what each one really wants and needs. Then, you will know how to develop an approach that fits."

"That is exactly what I do," said the salesman. "What you have just observed is my approach for a sales manager. It works almost every time." This young man had organized his method to fit the situation.

The Effective Church Series will follow that pattern in providing practical methodology for churches of every size and setting. Eagerness to articulate universal principles will not override the necessity of applying them to different situations in seemingly contradictory ways.

The Effective Church Series is not theology or Bible study, but its "ideas that work" rest on biblical principles. Without that basis, method sharing feeds us a diet of cotton candy, sweet but devoid of nutrients. Three verses from Proverbs form the three-legged biblical stool on which this book and the entire Effective Church Series will sit. "Where there is no vision, the people perish" (29:18 KJV). "Without counsel plans go wrong" (15:22). "An intelligent mind acquires knowledge, and the ear of the wise seeks knowledge" (18:15).

Teachers of Victorian literature tell this story about Thomas Carlyle. He was dressed to go out for a Sunday speech before a large crowd. His mother was sitting beside the front door. As Carlyle passed her on his way out, she said to him, "And where might you be going, Thomas?"

"Mother," he replied, "I'm going to tell the people what is wrong with the world."

His mother responded with, "Aye, Thomas, but are you going to tell them what do about it?"

These volumes will tell what is right about the church as well as what is wrong, and what to do about both.

Herb Miller
Lubbock, Texas

13

INTRODUCTION

When we get behind all the economic and political analysis, we finally recognize that the real problem in this social order is that there are not enough leaders to stand out in front and do the jobs that need to be done.

George Roche III,
President, Hillsdale College

A pastor attended a continuing education seminar for senior ministers of larger congregations. At coffee break, participants milled about, talking with one another. In the midst of the chatter, someone posed an important question to the nationally known church consultant conducting the event. "What will it take to turn around the decline of my church and my denomination?"

The pastor doubted that the consultant would choose to respond. Surely, the answer was so long and complex that it would occupy the remainder of the seminar. He was surprised when the consultant barely hesitated, yet gave a very serious reply: "That's easy. The answer is *leadership*. We need effective leaders to head our denominations and to be ministers in our congregations."

In recent decades, most ministers have not thought of themselves as the congregation's leaders. We have preferred such constructs as pastor, prophet, teacher, counselor, theologian, and preacher. True to the training many had during the 1960s, ministers might from time to time admit to "enabling the membership in its ministry." But that is ordinarily as close as they come to seeing their role of pastor as one of leadership. More recently, however, research is beginning to help us understand that local church ministers lead. To be effective in ministry and mission, congregations need more than caring pastors, compelling preachers, insightful prophets, and wise teachers. They must have ministers who lead.

Although the church's mission is different, in one way it is not different from other political, economic, and social institutions: It hungers for leadership. Hundreds of books and thousands of articles have supported this thesis. Yet what does that mean for local church ministry? Can any ordained minister learn to lead, or does it take special gifts? How does an effective leader differ from an efficient manager?

Vital church leaders meet the ten criteria described in the chapters of this book. These ten criteria transcend what is popularly thought of as "leadership style." Effective pastors utilize many different styles to achieve leadership status.

As might be anticipated, several assumptions form the foundation for this list of criteria for the vital church leader.

First assumption: The minister serves as the primary congregational leader. Laity, of course, can and should participate in leadership to their fullest potentials. However, the health of a congregation rises or falls based on the levels of commitment and competence of its minister, and on the quality of the relationship established between that person and the members of the church. Study the fifty-year history of any congregation. When plotting numerical, financial, outreaching, and programmatic "highs," almost without exception, one discovers that these times came when the church was served by its most effective ministers. And leadership skills made those ministers effective. Take this research one step further by tracking other ministries of those same pastors. Again, almost without exception, one discovers that ministers who are effective in one congregation are effective in others. As a midwestern denominational executive put it, "If I took the ministers from our ten most dynamic congregations and put them in ten other churches, I am certain the same thing would happen all over again. The primary issue is not the building and its location, not whether the community is growing, not advertising, and not how the church is organized. The issue is leadership, and the minister leads."

Second assumption: All ordained persons have at least a minuscule amount of leadership ability. Those without any ability are, supposedly and prayerfully, eliminated by the denominational processes through which persons must pass to enter the office of ordained clergy. Experience and research have demonstrated, however, that training and education can significantly improve this spiritual gift of leadership.

Third assumption: Ministers who lead have a strong sense of calling to pastoral ministry. They believe God chose them to make a difference in the church and in the lives of the people who make up the church. As John 15:16 puts it, Christ says, "You did not choose me; I chose you, and appointed you to go and bear much fruit, the kind of fruit that endures" (TEV). This call to ministry provides the strength to endure the demands of leadership in a local congregation.

Fourth assumption: An effective pastor uses his or her gifts "for the equipment of the saints, for the work of the ministry, for building up the body of Christ" (Eph. 4:12).

Fifth assumption: The *type* of leadership is as important as the quality of leadership. James MacGregor Burns identifies two basic types of leadership: the transactional and the transforming.[1] The transactional leader works by exchanging one thing for another: jobs for votes or subsidies for campaign contributions. In the church, a transactional leader might suggest the availability of God's grace in exchange for a healthy contribution, or encourage people to unite with the church as a way to enhance their social standing and to build the pastor's evangelism record.

A transforming leader, as described by Burns, recognizes the deepest needs of humankind and seeks to meet those needs by engaging the full personhood of followers. Ultimately, transforming leaders become moral agents. This kind of leadership relies on a relationship of mutual needs, aspirations, and values between the leader and the people led to produce positive changes in individuals and society. Transforming leadership is more appropriate for church leaders than transactional leadership. Ministry better concerns itself with helping others realize their potential as God's children than with making the pastor a more popular person. To be deemed faithful, ministry must be other-centered rather than self-centered. It must aim to satisfy higher needs rather than contenting itself with responding to the wants of lower urges. To be called an effective, faithful pastor, one must seek to do what is morally and theologically right, even when another course might be easier.

Sixth assumption: Where this kind of leadership occurs, the saints are equipped, the Church does ministry, and the body of Christ is built.

Seventh assumption: It is possible to be faithful, effective, and successful as a leader in the Church of Jesus Christ.

What can establish the future or reverse the decline of any congregation? The answer is the same thing required to make any kind of denomination or organization effective in any of the many purposes to which God calls it: leadership, the pearl without price.

I

LEADERS LEAD PEOPLE

Leaders mobilize the best in their followers, who in turn demand more from their leaders.

James MacGregor Burns,
New York Times,
November 1978.

The Search Committee at the Church of the Good Shepherd now faced the difficult task of replacing its retiring pastor, Dr. Bill Johnson. The members gathered for their first meeting and wrestled with the issue of pastoral skills. "We have agreed," Sally, the committee chair, said, "that this congregation has grown in numbers and finances to the point where we can easily call a leading preacher to our pulpit."

"That's right," Larry chimed in, "we are a leading congregation. In the past two years our evangelism record surpassed every other congregation in our district. To continue that growth, we must have great preaching on Sunday mornings."

"Let's not forget the capital campaign this spring," the

ever practical church trustee, Harvey Martin, interjected. "We want someone who will lead us in paying off the debt on the new building. Our new minister must be an organized administrator for that campaign to be successful. In addition, I want us to have a pastor who will be a recognized community leader. You know, like Dr. Barstow at First Community. In fact, most of us thought Bill Johnson had that reputation."

Since the hour was late, Sally sought to bring the meeting to a conclusion. "Then we agree. We want our next minister to be a strong leader. We will meet again next Tuesday to consider some names. Larry, would you close our meeting by leading us in prayer."

Obviously, members of this Search Committee use the word *leader* in different ways. Some think of *leading* and *growing* as interchangeable terms. For others, "leading preacher" suggests a high degree of homiletic competence. Harvey, the trustee, equates administration with leadership, and then proceeds to use the term a different way by defining "community leader" as a highly respected person. When Sally asks Larry to "lead in prayer," she suggests that leaders take the responsibility for doing certain things.

While touching the fringe of the term, each of these definitions dances around the central meaning of leadership. In the congregation, the minister must be more than able manager, respected doer, competent person, insightful prophet, and caring pastor. The pastor must be a leader, and that means moving, inspiring, and mobilizing the people of God for mission and ministry.

More than holding office, church leaders perform a function. They gather God's people for the task of bringing others into touch with the healing power of the Gospel of Jesus Christ. For this to happen, a leader must have a following.

Consider the plight of Jim. He was depressed. He had been pastor at Third Church for five years. The congregation had been declining long before he came. Nothing in his tenure halted that trend. At one time three hundred people of all ages had attended worship weekly. Now barely thirty, primarily elderly persons, gathered to struggle through the liturgy. The people did not consider Jim to be the problem. The congregation loved him. They believed him to be the finest pastor in the church's history. He did not, however, seem to have the ability to attract a following of new members.

"I thought it was coming," Jim lamented. "The trustees voted to close the church at the end of the year. Only the endowment kept us going for the past decade. Now, even that can't pay for the new roof that we need.

"Can you believe it? This will be the third congregation I closed since my ordination twenty years ago. I seem to have developed a specialized ministry—holding the hands of churches as they die!"

What Mother Teresa does for the destitute of Calcutta, Pastor Jim does for congregations. He keeps them comfortable until they die. That skill, combined with his warm personality and caring pastoral style, may eventually qualify him for sainthood, but it does not make him a leader. Unless his compassion is bolstered by complimentary gifts, his skills fall short of leadership. By definition, leaders lead people.

Once they have gathered a following, strong leaders get people to do more and be more than might otherwise seem possible. Business sources frequently tell the story of Federal Express. Its founder, Fred Smith, was a student at Yale when he wrote a paper about his dream of setting up a service that would guarantee overnight mail delivery. His professor gave his paper a C and told him that the concept was "interesting, but not in the real world."

Today Federal Express delivers more than 400,000 packages every twenty-four hours. Before the company met with success, however, they frequently nudged failure. Debt and litigation were integral to their corporate experience.

Total failure was avoided, in part, by the efforts of

the company's employees. Fred Smith inspired tremendous loyalty among them. In the desperate early days, some van drivers pawned their watches to buy gasoline in order to get deliveries to the airport on time.

In an age characterized by declining employee loyalty, what was different at Federal Express? A socio-psychological study concluded that this corporation was set apart from the norm by the leadership of Fred Smith. He had an ability to get common people to do uncommon things.[1]

Effective church leaders possess this same quality. When pastors actually function as leaders, they can say, "Let's do that!" and people follow. This quality can generate unexpected and remarkable results. Dying congregations experience new spiritual life. Creative programming flowers where once only stagnation existed. Despair about the present translates into hope for the future.

Building a Legacy of Leadership

Not only must a pastor gather and inspire a following, but she also must move new people into places of leadership so that the work of the church can continue.

Pastor Ginn did not understand this function of the pastor as leader. As a new seminary graduate, she accepted a call to a flourishing new congregation in the suburb of a large city. In her desire to make the gospel socially relevant, she never missed an opportunity to denounce an injustice or to witness before the larger community.

Her congregants considered themselves reasonably open to their minister's activities, but they never felt included. They also felt she neglected them and their needs. She regularly missed scheduled committee meetings at church in order to make public statements before the city council. Shut-ins went unvisited and visitors unrecognized. The Sunday sermon usually revealed the issues that had occupied the minister's time and thoughts that week. Almost always the people left morning worship feeling scolded for who they were and what they owned.

Four years after Ginn's arrival, the few who remained members decided to disband the congregation and sell the property. Ginn believed this the unavoidable consequence of her faithfulness to a prophetic ministry. When she felt called to another mission field, no one remained to carry on her work. While many members of the congregation understood her commitments and many even sympathized with them, none followed in their pastor's footsteps. The social activity she conducted on behalf of the congregation was not owned by the people.

Ginn, like Jim, the Comforter of the Dying, neglected the first principle of leadership: build a following. Ginn's very just concern to be prophetic was followed to the exclusion of the equally important responsibility to maintain congregational health. Her ministry differed from Jim's only in practicing euthanasia rather than awaiting congregational death from natural causes.

Despite her claims, the congregation Ginn served did not disband because her ministry was prophetic rather than pastoral. It died because she *failed to lead* both as pastor of the congregation *and* as prophet to the community. As a result, the congregation closed and her witness to the larger community ceased. She had not trained or inspired anyone to continue the work of the local church nor her witness to the larger community. When she left, there was no evidence that she had traveled that way.

Prophets may frequently function as solitary figures. As Bernard of Clairvaux said, "Learn the lesson that, if you are to do the work of a prophet, what you need is not a scepter but a hoe." Pastors, on the other hand, can never work successfully alone. Pastors as leaders gather a following, teach people how to do the job, and then inspire them to greater heights than they ever experienced. In doing so, the able leader leaves behind a record of accomplishment. Where no followers were gathered and none remain to carry on the work, there has been no leadership. Effective leaders leave tracks. Their imprint is evident in the spiritual health of both congregation and individuals.

In John 14:12, Jesus predicts that those who believe in him not only will ably follow in his footsteps but also will be able to do even greater things. This possibility holds for those whom God calls to ministry today. We strive to leave behind followers who do the job even better.

As one effective pastor explained, "I am now serving my fourth congregation since graduating from seminary. Each of the first three experienced significant growth during my tenure.

"I did not really function as leader, however, in the first two churches. Soon after I left, each shrank back to the same size and began to contend with the same problems they had before I came. I was not so much a leader as a performer. People came to the church to listen to me preach, but not necessarily to follow the teachings of Jesus Christ or to become active in the church.

"By the third congregation, I had things straight. I knew the difference between a performer's following and a leader's. While serving my third church, I trained other people and moved them into places of leadership. We implemented a shepherding program as well as developed ongoing procedures for recruiting, training, and motivating lay leaders. In the year that I resigned, over 50 percent of the members were involved in small groups for weekly prayer, Bible study, and other spiritual growth disciplines. When I left that congregation, they continued to grow numerically and spiritually. The minister who followed me never faltered. The congregation quickly accepted her and her ministry. I am thrilled. I really did the job right for them."

Getting People to Get Things Done

Leaders influence people's beliefs and their behaviors. Those who do not realize or accept the power of this influence can damage the people and/or the institution.

Therefore, do not undertake the role ill-advisedly. Leadership involves responsibility for getting people to do things.[2]

This smacks of manipulation and may seem to be inappropriate clergy behavior. Unfortunately, no reasonable alternative exists. By its very nature, ministry involves influencing belief and behavior. Fortunately, Christian ministry has noble intentions. We practice ministry for several good reasons. Among these reasons is our inclination toward raising humankind to its highest potential for good. The power we are called to exercise encourages rather than manipulates; it creates rather than corrupts. The good possibilities for influencing behavior and belief necessitate taking risks.

We should not, however, underestimate the immense power that ministers have, nor fail to see the temptation inherent in this capacity to influence.[3] People want to please us, and that leaves open great potential for abuse. Pastoral leadership must be alert to the necessity of modeling Christian morality. We are called to love people and use things, not to use people and love things. Faithful leadership must call forth the very best in humankind for service to God. Stroking a pastoral ego should never be the objective.

A pastor can be thought of as having the same relationship to the people of God as the shepherd has to the sheep. Shepherds love their sheep, see to it that their needs are met, and take responsibility for them. This inspires a trust that is similar to the trust that a congregation must have in their pastor.

Two men were watching a man drive a herd of sheep through the main street of a small town. "I thought shepherds led sheep. I didn't know they drove them with a whip."

"They do," the other fellow remarked. "That's not a shepherd. That's the town's butcher."

Ministers, like shepherds, lead. They do not drive. The Bible teaches that God's leaders set an example (I Pet. 5:3). They lead by kindness, gentleness, and patience (II Tim. 2:24-26). They also see leadership as a means to serve (Luke

22:24-27). Even though we seek to build a following, we do not lead by whipping the congregation into doing what we want when we want it. The skilled leader sets up situations in which others are willing to follow and are happy to work with her. The church's leaders demonstrate this skill by interpreting and applying biblical principles through thoughtfulness, enthusiasm, and sharing responsibility with others.

Beware These Stumbling Blocks

On a kitchen wall was a beautifully taxidermied sea gull with wings stretched as if in full flight. The wooden board on which the bird was mounted read, "Whenever *I* try to fly, someone stands on my wings."

Local church ministers frequently experience this frustration. Most congregations have at least a short list of folks who are like the elderly man who said, "In my life I have seen thousands of changes, and I have been against every one of them."

Wise leaders anticipate frustrations from people and from circumstances beyond their control. Maintaining sufficient energy to deal with these inevitable problems, however, requires that some of the unnecessary obstacles be eliminated. This includes the problems many clergy cause for themselves.

Consider the following a partial list of the obstacles to leadership that many clergy unnecessarily put on themselves.

Beware the Bog of Excessive Planning and Theologizing. All leadership requires planning, and a minister expects planning to have theological authenticity. However, as the nonbiblical proverb holds, "Whenever there is a good idea, someone will take it too far." Many great ideas have been planned or theologized to death.

Sam Billingsley, the chair of the Membership Committee at Old First Church, had a vision. He proposed that the congregation be organized into small caring groups for mutual ministry. This program of shepherding was given the name "Operation Love."

The committee loved the idea. The congregation was excited. Ten months and thirty meetings later the committee had written a manual, produced an administrative flow chart, and developed lists of families who would belong to each of the fifty-eight neighborhood groups. When completed, all of the manuals were stored on library shelves and the project died. Operation Love became an ecclesiastical albatross—too big and clumsy to get off the ground and fly. Unwittingly, the committee had fallen into the swamp of excessive planning and insufficient action. As Theodore Roosevelt expressed it, "I believe in men who take the next step, not those who theorize about the one-hundredth step."

Effective leaders plan without speculating on every probable and potential problem. They know the difference between leading and only thinking about leading.

One of the most damaging obsessive-compulsive behaviors is seen in pastors who get bogged down in theological contingencies. While ministers must work within and be guided by a framework of belief, church leadership can be self-limited by too much theological reflection (even though some of our theological mentors are convinced that we do not do enough careful theological thinking).

Clergy couple Sue and Randy engage in a continual debate on the relative merits of the church growth movement versus the ministry committed primarily to social justice. Randy considers himself the family prophet. Sue believes that evangelism is the highest priority. They spend so much time and energy researching Scripture and significant theologians to support their positions that neither accomplishes much in evangelism or social justice.

Engaging in either/or discussions on social justice and evangelism is similar to debating that only "heads" or only "tails" constitutes a coin. Our Christian faith requires both social justice and evangelism. How can we say that we believe if we don't put our faith into action? And if we really believe, would we not be anxious to share it in a persuasive manner?

Careful planning and theological reflection will keep one

27

on the right track. However, as Will Rogers said, "Even if you are on the right track, you'll get run over if you just sit there." Effective pastoral leadership seeks more than the survival of the local congregation. It also recognizes that without survival, accomplishing other objectives is extremely difficult.

Don't Do Things for Your Benefit. Hospital rooms are typically designed for the convenience of staff, not the comfort of the patient. Patients larger than the typical nine-year-old find the bed too narrow. This narrow design makes it possible for the physician to conduct examinations without stretching. Serious damage can be inflicted if one falls from such a tall bed. But the height makes it convenient for the nurse to take a patient's pulse and temperature. The typical hospital room has the lighting capacity of a presidential news conference. Though this light is painful to the patient, the staff needs the light to do its work.

Though such practices are acceptable in professional medicine, clergy cannot organize the local congregation for their personal and professional benefit. Not all meetings can be scheduled for the convenience of the pastor. The program cannot be shaped to fit the minister's interests. The mission of the congregation cannot be determined by what will look best on the pastor's resumé.

Sometimes You Must Take Charge. Although effective leaders involve others in the decision-making process, they also accept that the obvious must sometimes be done without extensive consultation. As one colleague put it, "I have come to realize it is often easier to be forgiven than to get permission."

One of the most frustrating weeks of one pastor's ministry was spent as a counselor at a junior high summer camp. The director began the week by bringing sixty youths into a circle and asking them, "What do *you want* to do this week?" Since these children had little previous experience making decisions about how to use their time and no experience at church camp, they did not know what they wanted to do. This non-directive approach resulted in six days of chaos.

Comedian Mel Brooks tells the story of a man named John who had a maddening compulsion to tear paper. After years of psychoanalysis, John was still tearing paper, and his family was losing hope. They finally took him to a new therapist. This fellow walked with John around the room and talked quietly to him. When John left the office, he was cured.

A year later, John's compulsion had not returned. The grateful family asked the therapist what he had said to John. The therapist responded, "I told him, 'Don't tear paper!' "

Leading sometimes means taking charge in order to say what must be said. A compulsion to ponder the obvious can be as much a pitfall as over-planning and action-free theologizing.

Be Ready to Explain the Obvious. The restroom in a popular restaurant was remodeled and a new paper towel dispenser was installed. The towels in the new dispenser were on a roll rather than individual sheets. After the dispenser was torn off the wall a few times by frustrated customers, the manager pasted a tiny picture diagram on the front accompanied by the words, "Turn handle in this direction."

That manager exhibited leadership. He understood more clearly than some pastors that people require instruction in the most simple matters. In the local church, be prepared to train people to do even simple tasks. Have an annual seminar on serving communion—even when the procedure has not changed since 1845. Don't assume that committee chairs know how to conduct a meeting or set goals and accomplish them. Remember, the first sentence on a road to failure begins, "Well, I assumed. . . . "

Be Ready for Interruptions. The pilot of a Boeing 747 rules absolutely. When he or she sits at the controls of the airplane, passengers, crew, and control tower staff pledge total cooperation. The pilot's clear responsibility is to get the plane safely to its destination. Only equipment failures and acts of nature should stand in the way of accomplishing this objective.

Local church leaders are more like jugglers than jet pilots. Rather than focusing on a single task, the typical minister's day begins with an interruption and then becomes a series of interruptions which are interrupted by interruptions. Funerals take precedence over planning meetings. Pastoral care emergencies alter study and reflection schedules. A snow storm cancels the Christmas Eve pageant, which took ten hours of rehearsal.

Effective local church leaders must adapt to whatever comes up and still accomplish their objectives. Those who do not adapt will find ministry a swamp.

Leadership and the "I" Factor

Former coach of the Washington Redskins, George Allen, once described the mysterious quality that all leaders have. On a television show he said something to this effect: "Never mind how many passes he throws and what his completion percentage looks like. My quarterback's got to be the guy who can take you in for a score in the last two minutes, when it's getting dark, the fans are down on you, the wind is blowing, and there's so much ice on the ball he can't grip it. A quarterback who can leave them for dead in two minutes."

Some ministers have this same ability. They manage to get things done under the most adverse circumstances. All of the parishes they serve flourish. People follow their lead. They establish a parish climate in which the membership grows spiritually by better coping with fear, by becoming more aware of dependence upon God, by fostering a more realistic appraisal of human frailties and strengths, by engendering compassion, and by showing people how to experience greater meaning and significance in their daily lives.[4]

Effective leaders radiate a sense of self-confidence and

authenticity. They believe in themselves and in their ability to get things done.[5] Their sense of moral rightness combines with technical competence to give them a soundness of character, which makes them attractive to others. We might call this the *Integrity* or *"I" Factor*.

Some people lead naturally. The "I" Factor was present at birth and grew like a flower in a tropical rain forest. Some people have no natural leadership ability at all. No matter how much they try, no matter how much leadership training they receive, they never get the hang of it. Most of us are between these extremes. We are born with some ability and must work hard to develop the "I" Factor present in us.

II

LEADERS GATHER PEOPLE AROUND A VISION

No wind blows in favor of a ship that has no direction.

Michel Eyquem de Montaigne, 1533–1592

Effective pastoral leadership requires dynamic double vision. Ministers require a passionate vision of a personal mission and a compelling vision for the congregation. While related and interdependent, these two visions should not be confused.

The Pastor's Vision for Ministry

Phillips Brooks told the story of going with a friend to hear a famous orator. As they left the auditorium, Brooks noticed that his friend had become silent. Soon the man asked Brooks, "Did you see where his power lay? What drives that man?"

That question caused Brooks to look beyond the enjoyment of a great sermon to ponder the source of the preacher's dynamism. What enables some people to achieve far beyond most of their contemporaries? Where do they find the extra reserve? Why do a few leave indelible footprints? How can others tap the needed inner resources in order to meet worthy goals of their own?

The source of that preacher's power was, of course, his commitment to the Christian faith. He was convinced of the basic affirmations of the Gospel. With heart and mind he believed that God's love, as revealed in Jesus Christ, can transcend the divisions imposed by history to unite all people as brothers and sisters. In spite of the human tendency to think otherwise, that preacher contended for the effectiveness of forgiveness over vengeance. Because the man believed that the universe was created by a loving and good God, he was absolutely certain that people should and could treat one another with fairness and justice. This personal vision dwelt at the center of his life, calling forth and shaping everything he did. He also felt called to spend his life telling others that they would benefit from knowing and believing the same Gospel which set the direction for his life.

People who accomplish significant deeds are usually driven by a vision to which they are totally committed. Dr. Jonas Salk discovered the first vaccine against polio. Of that scientific effort, he offers this reflection: "Ideas came to me as they do to all of us. The difference is I took them seriously. I didn't get discouraged that others didn't see what I saw. I didn't allow anyone to discourage me—and everyone tried. But life is not a popularity contest."[1]

Vision drives effective ministerial leaders as well as famous scientists. A commitment to the basic tenets of the Gospel can provide unrelenting optimism, unflappable confidence, and unstoppable drive. Effective pastors permit nothing to stop their pursuit of their vision for ministry. Their confidence in Christ empowers their drive toward what might be.

All pastors have a concept of ministry (or a personal mission statement) that serves as their guiding vision. These internal guidance systems are revealed when you ask questions such as the following: "What are you called to do in ministry? What keeps you going through the tough times? What drives you?"

Responses vary greatly. Ministers trained in the 1960s often consider themselves primarily pastoral counselors, and their style of ministry tends to depend on their listening skills. Those who lean toward the prophetic engage in ministry primarily to affect social and political change. Others, weathered by the strong winds of a late twentieth-century business model, conduct themselves primarily as managing directors of a religious organization. Regrettably, a few limit both their vision for and practice of ministry to leading tours to the Holy Land or hanging on until retirement.

What one believes about ministry determines the way one practices it. One pastor conducted an informal survey among ministers whom he considered effective leaders. The retired chief executive of a mainline denomination said, "I do ministry as a way to serve humanity. I want to influence the most people possible, and I want to do that by serving others rather than by being served."

A local church pastor with a bent toward social action reported, "I have always been haunted by the vision of the Christ with outstretched arms, beckoning, 'Be more like me.' I spend my ministry haunting the church with that same vision."

The pastor of an extremely large congregation who considers himself primarily a preacher said, "I am the mouthpiece for the Gospel. I put the fire under the kettle of the authoritative, existential, experiential Word of God."

The pastor of a smaller but significantly growing congregation, who has a reputation for being particularly effective at implementing church growth principles, describes his ministry as "devoted to bringing individuals into the community of faith."

A pastor who considers herself more of an evangelist said, "I am foremost in the business of bringing people into touch with the healing touch of the Gospel." Indeed, it seems that pastors conduct themselves according to their visions.

A great preacher once told a story of a group of boys

standing along the banks of the flooded Tennessee River. About two hundred yards off shore, a stack of lumber jutted out of the water. On the lumber a terrified rabbit had found safety.

One of the boys, knowing how water frightens rabbits, decided to try to capture it and have it for dinner. He found a canoe and paddled into the swollen river. As expected, the rabbit was more frightened of the water than of the boy and consequently was captured, killed, and stuffed into a jacket pocket.

Unfortunately, the young man was not a very good canoeist. He capsized and drowned. It took three days to recover the body. When the body was found, one of the fellows who had witnessed the episode pulled what remained of the rabbit from the boy's pocket. He held it into the air and announced, "This is what he gave his life for."[2]

Pastoral ministry demands total commitment. We give our lives for the church, and our vision determines how we live out that commitment. For this reason, not only must our vision lead us to do worthwhile tasks, but we also had best feel a strong call to ministry. Believing "I do this because God has called me" helps make it possible to survive the tough times.

Ingredients in a Congregation's Vision

By study, reflection, experience, and experimentation, the effective clergy person develops a clearly articulated, theologically sound, and passionately held vision for personal ministry. The pastor as leader must also offer the congregation a vision to pursue. David Rockefeller once observed that "the number one function of the top executive is to establish the purpose of the organization."[3] Although the church and the business organization differ in many ways, pastors—like executives—lead. Both take responsibility for communicating visions. Without leadership to gather the congregation around an agreed upon purpose, the church fulfills the old dictum "If you don't know where you are going, any road will do."

Vision addresses the possibilities for congregational mission and ministry by offering a positive way to talk about the past and present. It also images what might be in such a specific, attainable way that change can be perceived as a worthwhile possibility. Most important, congregational vision must be more than reasonable and socially relevant. It must be theologically sound.

First, a compelling vision appraises the present reality positively. A wise minister never proposes change without listening carefully to members talk about their personal lives, their faith, and their church. How do people describe themselves? What does the church believe is the best it has to offer? A road map for the future cannot be drawn without a thorough knowledge of the present location.

After gathering this critical information from the members, the wise pastor gives it a positive spin. This facilitates moving the people into the future. After all, people who feel good about themselves, their past, and their present more readily visualize a positive future than those who wallow in negative self-understanding.

Barry came to the Rolling Brook Church at a difficult time. Ten years before, the denomination skimped when buying property. The congregation had too little land and was five blocks off a main east-west thoroughfare. The members believed that they were "poor cousins" of the Cathedral Church two miles away. Low self-image and negative conversations among members of the congregation poisoned the well for visitors. The few who visited seldom returned. The congregation had locked themselves into a downwardly spiraling, self-fulfilling prophecy.

Barry, however, understood good leadership principles. After listening carefully to the people, he began to speak positively of their situation. "Our location is fine. Although we are not on College Avenue, we are close. And this church building is within fifteen minutes of nearly two-thirds of the people in this city. We don't have the wealthy folks they have at the Cathedral, but we have wonderful families. Rolling Brook Church has great potential." In Barry's eight-year ministry at Rolling Brook Church, the congregation doubled in size and quadrupled in self-esteem. A positive way to talk about past and present serves as the foundation for deciding how to move into the future.

Second, the best visions are specific and attainable. If the vision calls for evangelistic zeal, then "The World For Christ" resounds magnificently but suffers from both improbability and vagueness. On the other hand, "Seven Hundred More By 2004" can be measured and might be possible.

Third, a good vision makes moving toward the future seem a worthwhile possibility. Unless this criterion is met, few will feel compelled to follow. St. Mary's Church had an illustrious past and a meaningful present. They did not, however, have a plan for the future. Pastor Joanne Smith suggested that a well-known church consultant lead them in long-range planning. This recommendation was nearly rejected because of the program's name: *New Directions Conference.*

"Who says there is anything wrong with our present directions?" several prominent members argued. The disagreement was defused by changing the title of the program to *Parish Enrichment Conference!* The thought of enriching the church's program was much less threatening than moving in a new direction. The different name removed the negative implications about the present and made undertaking the program a worthwhile possibility. The people could throw their wholehearted support behind a program that suggested that the future could be even better than the present.

Those who expect to gather a following should never underestimate the power of the way things are stated. After all, if you asked the average person to stand in a very confined space with a small spherical missile flying around at 100 miles per hour, most would reply, "Are you crazy?" But if you asked, "Would you like to play racquetball?" the likelihood of a positive response increases dramatically.

Fourth, the best visions seek to be faithful to the gospel. The minister as leader gathers people to seek the will of God. This requires more than polling the congregation for what it would like to do. It also means that the agenda for the church's future should not be established simply by responding to a political and social agenda.

Additionally, faithful pastors do not gather people around themselves. They gather people around what God calls the Church to be. In fact, only those visions consistent with what the Creator wants are empowered.

To illustrate how to build a congregational vision, consider what happened at Old First Church. Their history paralleled the history of the mainstream denomination with which it was affiliated. The congregation had been declining in numbers and influence for two decades. To Jim Walker, the new Senior Minister, fell the responsibility of proposing something to get this congregation moving in a positive direction.

He used his "State of the Church" address at the board planning retreat to reveal the vision he had for congregational life and ministry. The board was surprised. Pastor Jim did not deliver the annual lecture on the need for more budget support and increased worship attendance. Nor did he make the usual plea for faithful attendance at monthly committee meetings. Instead, he suggested that the congregation begin thinking of the local church as a spiritual caravan. "After all," Jim said, "people in congregations and in frontier wagon trains share a common purpose. Both are communities of people who covenant to make a trip together—the journey west, or the one through life."

The pastor then analyzed the congregation's understanding of its ministry. Members thought of themselves, he told them, as an "ecclesiastical general store where a few clerks, namely the lay leadership and the minister, dispense religious goods and services to the members and the public. Everyone in town knows that Old First Church is a beautiful place for a wedding. The ordained staff can always be relied upon as community chaplains when the unchurched need a funeral. The ministers of this church have a long-standing and community-wide reputation as reliable counselors. Our Christmas Eve and Easter morning worship services draw crowds of people who never attend church regularly. Old First Church serves Oakdale as well as any old-fashioned general store served its community."

"There is nothing inherently wrong in being the Church of

the General Store," Jim explained. "In fact, we want to continue this ministry. We are good at it. However, there are many more possibilities in becoming the Church of the Spiritual Caravan. It offers a way for us to think dynamically about ourselves. We need a plan of action, and becoming a spiritual caravan will give us a way to start developing that plan."

Jim Walker undertook a primary responsibility for leadership. He offered a vision to the members of Old First Church. The "general store" and "spiritual caravan" images provided members with a positive way to understand both their past and present situations, as well as a hopeful way to move into a different future. He sought to offer a vision consistent with the mission of the church.

In the months that followed, Jim and the board members began to give specificity to the vision. Together, they delineated its implications for church planning, programming, mission, and ministry. The spiritual caravan imagery began to imprint as the board considered implications for numerical and spiritual growth, small group development, fellowship, and education. Old First Church was on the way to adopting a new vision of who they were and what they should be doing as a congregation.

Visions Describe and Determine Reality

By offering vision, leaders shape the thinking and, consequently, the doing of the congregation. The vision, therefore, not only describes the present but also points to the desired destination. By becoming the congregation's road map, the vision helps determine destiny as well as describe present reality.

The Australians incorporated this determining dimension of vision into their nation's coat of arms. It pictures an emu, a large flightless bird, standing with a kangaroo. These animals were chosen because they share a common characteristic—neither can move backward. If an emu, with its three-toed feet, tries to go backward, it falls over. The kangaroo is similarly handicapped by its long tail. Thus, these animals depict the spirit of Australia—never backward, always forward.[4]

Of course, this coat of arms does more than merely describe the Australian spirit. It helps to *determine* it as well. People who believe that they cannot move backward are more likely to value moving forward. Vision shapes behavior as well as describes it.

Prior to Jim's arrival, Old First Church prided itself on being a servant to the community. The congregation's ministry focused on finding ways to meet the religious needs of the community. Over the years, the entire church program revolved around this theme: "What Can We Do for Others?"

Although noble, even profoundly "Christian," this vision did not provide for the spiritual needs of the church's own membership. The people experienced life in the church as all "giving" and little "getting." New members were quickly assigned to one of the congregation's many projects, committees, or task forces. Within a short period of time, these people moved into leadership positions to replace those who were retiring from their responsibilities. Before long, the "new" member became exhausted and had to be replaced by an even newer member.

Old First Church's sense of mission was enviable, but the burnout rate undermined long-range hopes of continuing its mission. The people had too few channels for spiritual refueling. Jim's vision of the spiritual caravan provided a necessary corrective. Wagon train travelers, obviously, had ways to be fed—physically, spiritually, emotionally—as well as ways to serve the needs of one another. Jim's combination of the caravan and general store images gave the people a way to continue their outreach ministry while they pursued spiritual growth. The vision he offered both described and determined the congregation's reality.

The Leader's Role

The effective local church pastor spends an enormous amount of time and energy as "keeper of the vision." This includes generating the vision, rallying support for it, making adjustments to it, and repeating it over and over again until the vision becomes an integral part of the congregation's pattern of thinking and doing. Effective leaders take responsibility for the vision. Although the congregation must be consulted, committees do not generate visions. When vision-building becomes a process done only by the present structures, frustration results. Egalitarian group visions normally duplicate the status quo. The responsibility of codifying the vision falls to leadership, and in the local church the leader is the minister. The pastor collects, sorts, and codifies the data given by the membership. Then, while being both sensitive to the people and responsible to the Gospel, he or she offers an image of what might be.

The leader must repeat the vision over and over again. Changing the way churches think and do is comparable to writing instructions in a snowdrift during a blizzard. Every few minutes it must be done again. Pastors paint the vision during sermons, reports, committee meetings, and conversations with lay leaders. Over and over again, the leader says, "God calls us to do this, and we can do it."

III

LEADERS MOTIVATE PEOPLE

Most people want to do their very best job. In most organizations that doesn't happen because there are too many obstacles in the way. To help people excel, you have to remove as many obstacles as you can.

Roger Herman

During the district pastors' retreat, Pastor John tried to explain the problem to a colleague. "This congregation has lazy members. They don't want to do anything. Worship attendance has declined steadily since I arrived. Bible study groups continue to disband. Only a handful come to committee meetings. Even the last fellowship dinner was a failure.

"It bewilders me. I accepted the call to this congregation because it had the reputation for dynamic programming. When Harry Smith was pastor, the place was a beehive of activity. Maybe the people burned out. Maybe they don't have enough strength remaining to do anything. I sure wish someone would light a fire under them. I am getting tired of leading when no one follows."

Contrary to what John thinks, he has responsibility for

motivating the congregation. Followers do not normally light fires under themselves. Although there may be exceptions, congregational inactivity seldom results from the people's inability to follow an inspired leader. Inactivity must be traced elsewhere. God calls talented, committed people into every congregation. The church charges the pastoral leader with finding a way to motivate and mobilize the congregation to fulfill God's calling for ministry and mission.

Motivational Logjams

Imagine a river clogged by entangled timber. That logjam inhibits the stream's current, preventing the stream from flowing properly. The river must be unclogged. Motivating inactive congregations is a similar challenge. Both the stream's current and the congregation's potential for ministry and mission have been interrupted by obstacles.

There are several obvious solutions to the logjam. The logs could be unloosed by a well-placed charge of dynamite. Of course, an explosion might do more damage than good. The snarled timber might also be dislodged by removing individual logs, carrying them one at a time to open water, and floating them downstream. Eventually, the stream's current would be sufficient to break up the logjam. This method, while safer than dynamite, would require an enormous expenditure of personal energy.

Finding the most efficient way to dislodge a motivational logjam requires effective planning. First, calculate the power supplied by the stream's current. How can this available energy be maximized? Can it be increased by opening an upstream dam or lock?

Second, study carefully the pattern of the fallen timber. All logs do not contribute equally to the blockage. Take advantage of the river's current, and remove the logs that cause the jam.

Casey Stengel, former manager of the Yankees and the Mets, once observed that "It's easy to get good players. Gettin' 'em to play together, that's the hard part." Every pastor benefits from making the same assumption about the congregation that he or she serves. Congregations should be thought of as being filled with capable members who are struggling to find a better way to play together. The smallest, weakest church with the most aged membership still bubbles with possibility. Congregations have potential because of the universally high aspirations of the members.

The Church of Jesus Christ has always attracted people who are searching for a deeper meaning and a more positive direction for their lives. From the first century through the twentieth century, the church has been filled with highly motivated people. Today's Christians, like the first Christians, are dissatisfied with the ordinary. They want something more for themselves and their families. Christianity has always offered a channel for those with upwardly mobile aspirations.[1] The wise leader, therefore, can safely assume that Christians want to have an enriching church experience.

Be Alert to the Principle of Equilibrium. Every logjam seeks equilibrium. The perfectly arranged jam allows the stream's current to pass through its structure without significantly altering the jam itself. The jam is designed to handle whatever pressure the stream offers. If new logs collect on the upstream side of the jam, then the jam compensates by setting a few logs free on the downstream side. Eventually, the jam reestablishes equilibrium. Logjams are studies in making adjustments without making major changes.

Organizations, including congregations, also tend to seek equilibrium. By nature, congregations seem to structure themselves to resist most shifts in the theological breeze, changes in denominational polity, and ideas suggested by the pastor. Like logjams in the river, congregations have an established way to channel the current without having to make major changes.

The wise pastor studies the congregation as carefully as the lumberjack studies the logjam. He or she must gather knowledge about how energy flows through the church. If nothing important seems to be happening, then the congregation has established equilibrium. How has the church structured itself to make this happen? Who makes decisions? Who blocks decisions? Those who fail to gather this information may be tempted to try dynamiting the congregation into action.

Pastor Sally scolded and pleaded. Finally, in desperation born of inexperience, she threatened to resign if the church board failed to adopt her recommendation for a congregational shepherding program. Since the program involved an expenditure of several hundred dollars, the board tabled the proposal. Within a week, the congregation was split on whether or not Sally should resign. The controversy was so divisive that the congregation never acted on the shepherding program which nearly everyone thought was a great idea.

Had Sally more carefully studied the congregation's informal ways of thinking and doing, she would have realized that the board never voted on expenditures until it knew how Uncle Jack Johnson, a church trustee for fifty years, felt about the matter. No one could remember why he was given so much authority, but he had it. His judgment served as the final word on financial matters.

Since Uncle Jack was absent from the meeting, regular board members knew the issue must be tabled. Sally, who was new not only to this congregation but also to pastoral ministry, did not realize that the church was structured in a way that made Uncle Jack responsible for approving all financial decisions. Even Uncle Jack did not realize the key role he played in the congregation's operation, nor did he ever become personally aware of it. But he had veto power over all financial matters. By nature he was an agreeable fellow. He probably would have wholeheartedly supported the program and the expenditure it would require. Sally's threat to resign, however, exploded like dynamite in the midst of the congregation.

Six months later things settled down. Equilibrium was restored. Sally apologized for her rash threat to resign. The congregation once again was talking about the need for a shepherding program. Uncle Jack thought that the program Sally proposed was the best. To her credit, Sally learned a valuable lesson from the experience. The key to getting anything done at this church was getting Uncle Jack involved.

Inactive congregations have established equilibrium. They have structured themselves to adjust to shifting pressures without making major changes. Rather than condemning this as immoral, the effective leader accepts this as the reality with which one must deal.

Most congregations have one or more Uncle Jacks (or Aunt Janes). These people cue the congregation's ways of thinking and doing. One minister reports that at each church council vote the under-forty group turns to see how George is voting. The over-forties strain to watch Paul and then follow his lead.

Aunt Jane and Uncle Jack may be "yes" or "no" people. "No" folks have the power to veto, but they do not necessarily need to approve something. If they say, "Well, I am not opposed," then the congregation feels free to act. One does not, however, have to acquire their positive support. "Yes" folks, on the other hand, approve decisions. They must be enthusiastic or the idea will fizzle. The effective leader understands that the congregation might be set free by alleviating a "no" person's reservations or by spending a little extra time getting a "yes" person to understand the benefits of an idea.

Keep in mind that Aunt Jane and Uncle Jack may not be members of the official decision-making body of the church. Their influence may be derived from having once served as officers, from being members of a leading family in the community, or from annually contributing a large part of the budget. Uncle Jack or Aunt Jane may or may not be problems to solve. They are, however, always powers with whom to reckon. Identifying them provides insight into how the congregation functions. Knowing how they attained their positions provides clues to how to create growth and effectiveness in the congregation's ministry. Effective pastoral leaders, however, make it a priority to identify and work with the Uncle Jacks and Aunt Janes of the congregation. These people are key to what happens or does not happen in every congregation.

Common Congregational Obstructions

Pastor John, who complains that he cannot even "bring off" a successful fellowship dinner, should think of his unmotivated congregation as logjammed, not lazy. John needs to dislodge those obstacles that keep the congregation from flowing smoothly. Since the congregation has a history of significant activity, he can safely assume that sufficient energy still flows through the congregation to do effective ministry.

Thus far, John's attempts to motivate have been limited to whining about the congregation's lethargy. Constant complaining contributes to the logjam rather than releasing energy for ministry. He needs to study more carefully the congregation's ways of doing and thinking in order to determine what keeps them from being as active as they were during the previous pastor's tenure. Then, with great care, he must see what he can do to minimize or eliminate those obstacles. Even though each congregation is unique, many congregations face similar obstacles.

The Congregation May Not Understand the Gospel. Our faith calls us to forgive rather than to seek revenge; to understand how much more blessed it is to give than to receive; to wage peace, not war; and to use things and love people. The present age encourages us to watch out for "numero uno," to never hesitate to unload our hate or anger on others, and to love things and use people. It should not be surprising that well-intentioned church folk accept the values of the culture instead of the teachings of the faith. Unfortunately, the Gospel is a mystery to many Christians.

Ignorance of basic faith principles keeps some congregations from realizing their potential. Systematic biblical instruction combined with a program of regular preaching on the basics of faith may do a great deal to dislodge this obstacle. One must be careful, however, not to use Scripture as a bludgeon. Beating a congregation over the head is counter-productive. It only reinforces the system that maintains the status quo. Offered lovingly, the Gospel has amazing power for growth and change.

The Congregation May Lack a Positive Model for Being the Church. Some congregations have had little experience in being the Church. The key lay persons may have experienced church life only as responding to painful problems. They may have endured too many crises. Finances may be a long-term issue. They know no other goal than paying the bills. They may be paralyzed by worry for their aging membership and declining influence in the community.

Many congregations appear unmotivated because they do not understand how churches function as dynamic faith communities. They need appropriate models for being an effective congregation. Unfortunately, the supply is limited. Even when models are available, the congregation may choose an inappropriate model. Little Church on Side Street with its one hundred members cannot expect to model its program after First Mega Church. Little Church will never have a choir of one hundred or a youth group of three hundred. Believing that it should undermines whatever motivation the members have. The pastor who leads a congregation that is uncertain about how to be the Church will need to give considerable guidance if he or she expects the people to realize their potential.

The Congregation May Lack Structures for Being the Church. New Church has a problem. It grew to one hundred members the first year after it was established. Then it plateaued. Since it closed its charter six years ago, little has happened. Visitors come, attend a few weeks, and then drift away. They seldom join. The church neither developed nor communicated a policy on how people become members of New Church. Members might benefit from a new adult Sunday school class, but they have never determined how to start one. New Church has never developed a way to start a Bible study or a men's, women's, couples', or youth group. In fact, New Church has few ways to assimilate new members into groups, which explains why so few people become new members. New Church doesn't have officers because there is no election procedure. The members make consensus decisions in response to each catastrophe. New

Church, like many other congregations, has simply never established sufficient structures to make it possible for its members to function.

Consider the fable of the hippo who fell in love with the butterfly. He sought the advice of the wise old owl. "You must become a butterfly," the owl told the hippo, "and do it right now." The hippo was delighted. He plunged back into the jungle, only to return shortly. "How do I become a butterfly?" the hippo inquired of the owl. The bird of great wisdom responded, "That's up to you. I only set the policy. I don't implement."

Ministers cannot behave as owls. Pastoral leaders provide a vision for *what* might be, but they also provide nuts and bolts instruction for *how* to get things done. Ministers gain their know-how from personal experience, carefully selected continuing educational events, and the counsel of wiser, more experienced ministers. This practical knowledge may include anything from guidance on how to shape a committee's idea into a recommendation for a vote at the church council to establishing a procedure on how to start a new adult Sunday school class. When the congregation is in deadlock because it does not know how something should be done, the leader assumes the responsibility for removing the obstacle.

The Congregation May Not Know How to Short-circuit Conflict. For every congregation lacking structures and procedures for making decisions and accomplishing things, there is a congregation immobilized by its inability to resolve conflict. Without means to settle disagreements, these churches remain locked in their problems. By repeating the same painful history over and over again, such congregations manage to establish an equilibrium of misery.

First Church of Nit Picking and Squabbling has fired every pastor since 1926. Even those who managed to pastor this feisty flock for a decade or more ended their tenure on the short end of a vote of confidence. Key lay leaders of the church rank among the most committed, caring Christians of the age, but they have never been able to bring themselves to deal constructively with a few persistent gossips and nay-sayers. After a usually short but pleasant honeymoon period, these negative influences begin to spread malicious venom about the pastor. "She cannot preach very well." "Spends too much time with the youth." "He makes unannounced calls on housewives!" "I hear she rents dirty videos over in Smut City."

Sometimes the rumors become so persistent that people begin to believe that "where there is smoke, there must be fire." At other times, the maligned pastor becomes enraged. Reacting irrationally to the gossip or criticism, the pastor thereby undermines his or her credibility with the otherwise caring majority.

The next pastor frequently reloads the problem rather than resolves it. Instead of diagnosing repeated cycles of unresolved conflict, the next minister sympathizes with the people against the ghastly, unprofessional behavior of his or her predecessor. In an effort to build a base of support, this newly arrived clergy person may even become aligned with the negative element. By listening agreeably, even joyously, to the complaints and rehashed gossip, the minister permits the nay-sayers to avoid taking responsibility for their actions. This approves and thus reinforces the negative behavior.

Congregations like First Church of Nit Picking and Squabbling can repeat this cycle of clergy abuse endlessly. Leadership must extinguish these negative behaviors and help the congregation find ways to resolve conflict.

Ministers Significantly Impact Environment

The minister, more than any other individual, determines congregational environment. Influential laity frequently determine fiscal policy without seeking clergy input. Others in the congregation may make program decisions. Even when they long to do it, some clergy do not even get to select the hymns. But like it or not, the minister has enormous influence in determining if church life will be experienced as positive or negative, encouraging or discouraging, stifling or

51

exciting. Therefore, effective pastoral leaders strive to model attitudes and behaviors conducive to the healthiest congregational attitude.

Enthusiasm: A Vitalizing Vitamin. The United States government once conducted a study to determine why residents of Panama were sluggish. The study revealed that both plant and animal life in that area lacked B vitamins. This deficiency in an otherwise nutritious diet rendered the population listless. When thiamine was added to the people's diet, their energy levels increased dramatically.[2]

Some congregations suffer from a similar vitamin deficiency. In spite of committed memberships, strong governing policies, and a well-educated clergy, they accomplish little. These churches need to be injected with Vitamin E—for *enthusiasm*.

Clergy serve as the most available source of this activating ingredient. The Southern Baptist Convention studied what moves churches off plateaus. They discovered that 82 percent of "breakout" churches report that the ability to generate enthusiasm is the most important factor in their leadership. In growing churches, the pastor generates a sense that "something exciting is happening here." The pastor's enthusiasm becomes the excitement that the church feels.[3]

Pastors do well to remember that people are motivated more by the depth of one's conviction than the height of one's logic, and more by the leader's enthusiasm than his or her management skills. Therefore, effective leaders know that they must do more than carefully articulate a vision for the church. A leader must be excited about that vision. Congregations find a minister's enthusiasm contagious.

Of course, substance must undergird enthusiasm. The pastor's excitement must be theologically grounded, must arise from a positive vision of future possibilities rather than from fear of the present, and must be constructed on the encouragement of positive behaviors rather than on an attack on the values of others. Without these qualities, enthusiasm degenerates to a short-lived wind storm.

Fish with the Bait That Fish Like. "All the Buttermilk You Can Drink—One Dime!" Whenever the restaurant on the corner put that sign in its windows, little brother raced for his piggy-bank. He loved buttermilk and could drink carton after carton. The older brother, on the other hand, did not like buttermilk. The sign did nothing to attract his business. Unfortunately, they did not offer a special on chocolate milk. That would have interested him.

Leaders accept the fact that people respond in different ways to different things at different times in their spiritual journeys. People can be motivated by achievement, by recognition of their efforts, by challenging work, by responsibility, by personal growth, or by caring fellowship. A person who is new to town might join a certain church because of the warmth of the believing community. Five years later, he may continue to participate in that church because it offers a Bible study that continually renews his faith. After ten years, he may be strongly motivated by the challenge to be a lay leader.

Effective pastors are sensitive to these differing motivations. When designing a stewardship drive, for instance, they take into account the reality that some people respond well to the challenge of raising a budget bigger than last year's. Other people give because they appreciate the caring fellowship experiences that the church provides. Still others see growth in personal stewardship as a channel for spiritual growth. The most successful stewardship drives have multiple motivations and target various audiences.

Ineffective leaders ignore this principle in favor of trying to motivate by what motivates them. This is like fishing with bait that the fisherman likes rather than with bait that the fish like.

Responding to a variety of motivational stimuli requires that flexibility be a major construct in every pastor's method. While ministers can be reasonably productive with any leadership style, from autocrat to laissez-faire, none can be effective without a willingness to be flexible. John Wesley, a classic leader, changed his ways—sometimes almost against his will—in order to pursue his vision of a renewed church.

He did not want to use women as class leaders, but he did. He did not want to use lay preachers, but he did. He was reluctant to preach in open fields, but he made that a major element in his preaching ministry. Wesley understood that the climate for evangelism benefited from flexibility.

Like most great Christian leaders, Wesley remembered that it was not his job to twist arms to motivate people. Instead, Wesley wanted to create a climate in which people were set free to become the people God wanted them to be.

IV

LEADERS ENCOURAGE PEOPLE

*The primary job of the leader is appreciation. Other
tasks the leader may have must be regarded as trivial
in comparison to this.*

David Keirsey and Marilyn Bates,
Please Understand Me

Rose is serving her first parish, a small congregation
on the edge of town. At the monthly minister's meeting, she
initiated a conversation with one of the more experienced
pastors in the district. "Mary, there is something I don't
understand," she began. "I read Nick McWilliam's column in
his weekly newsletter. He spent nearly two paragraphs
thanking the members of Central Church for his vacation!
The way he went on, one might have thought the
congregation awarded him a three-year sabbatical to be
followed immediately by early retirement. What's the big
deal? Don't ministers usually receive a vacation as a fringe
benefit?"

"Rose," Mary answered, "Nick's thanking the congregation for vacation time typifies the way he does ministry. He
really appreciates the benefit. More than that, he is genuinely

thankful for the people of Central Church. He regularly writes thank-you notes to people who do routine tasks in the church. Unlike many of us, he doesn't take his job or the people for granted. In part, that may account for why he is considered to be one of the most effective ministers in this denomination. Giving thanks for a vacation contributes to the joyous atmosphere at that church. On your next free Sunday morning, worship there. You will feel the excitement as you walk in the door."

Sixty-year-old Nick McWilliams has been pastor of Central Church for nearly twenty years. During his tenure, the congregation has flourished. Despite its location in a declining downtown neighborhood, the membership has doubled. So many families with children have joined that the congregation's average age has dropped significantly. The congregation's reputation for its nurture and outreach programs extends far beyond the limits of the small city of 100,000. The entire denomination views Central Church as the model of the vital congregation.

Much of the credit goes to the beloved pastor, Nick McWilliams. He has mastered what has been called "The Greatest Management Principle in the World."[1] His style of ministry has created a positive climate in which people feel valued, successes are celebrated, and appreciation is freely given. Nick McWilliams follows in the footsteps of Barnabas, one who encourages (Acts 4:36). Nick understands and practices a ministry of giving a positive word to others.

Why Accentuate the Positive?

As mentioned in the previous chapter, effective leaders assume responsibility for congregational climate. The minister who wants to be productive strives to create an environment for ministry that can be described by adjectives such as positive, encouraging, achieving, valuing, succeeding, and healthy. Congregations with these energizing elements get things done. Congregations that lack these elements find that the doors to success have greased doorknobs.

A study conducted by the Southern Baptist Convention noted that membership-plateaued congregations lack confidence. Renewal requires that a positive attitude be instilled in order to elevate the congregation's level of confidence, commitment, and spirituality.[2] Leaders who advocate and practice a style of positive encouragement help their churches to get off the plateau.

Positive encouragement must be more than an adopted style of leadership. It must arise from the minister's deep love for the Church and care for the people of God. Fred Smith, Christian businessman and writer on leadership, draws a parallel between the pastor of a church and the conductor of an orchestra. Like the accomplished maestro, the effective pastor combines an awe for the composer, God, and an intimate knowledge of the score, the Bible. Both conductor and pastor set meaningful interpretive beats that make it possible for the congregation or the orchestra to play to their highest potentials.[3] The greatest effectiveness, however, is reserved for the conductor or pastor who can also communicate his or her sincere and deep appreciation for the orchestra or congregation and the music that they produce together. This inspires great performances.

Because It Is Sound Psychology. Few principles of modern psychology have a more unblemished track record than positive reinforcement. Since Pavlov clanged bells and fed canines, few have questioned that reward has a positive impact on behavior. What works in the kennels also works in the pews. People respond well to praise, appreciation, encouragement, and all other forms of positive reinforcement.

Unfortunately, leaders do not always take advantage of the benefits offered by positive reinforcement. Frequently we utilize negative reinforcement. Consider the cartoon of two scruffy grade school boys chatting on a street corner. One says to the other, "The teacher sent me home from school because I bit Johnny. I always bite Johnny when I want to go home."

Leadership in local congregations frequently encourages the ecclesiastical equivalent to "biting Johnny." We reward behavior that needs to be repudiated. Some clergy even seem to specialize in encouraging a negative climate. One congregation's pastoral visitor generated a minimum of three volatile conversations on denominational social action positions each week. Although this fellow insisted that he never instigated these discussions, neither the pastor nor any of the lay leaders encountered members who wanted to become embroiled in these bitter exchanges. Whether wittingly or unwittingly, the pastoral visitor generated a negative climate.

Pastors usually learn early in their ministries that negative people seldom need prompting. Every congregation has at least one person who complains about each change in the order of worship and usually at least two others who object to spending the church's money for building maintenance, world outreach, the pastor's salary, or other things that they consider frivolous. These people offer their opinions without invitation. If the leaders are not careful, a congregation can spend much of its precious time and energy responding to these squeaky wheels. When a negative minority is permitted to determine congregational life and ministry, the atmosphere becomes poisoned. Fortunately, a positive climate of encouragement provides the momentum to dislodge the grip of negative people.

Most people want to please the leader. In a climate of encouragement, people are motivated to follow. Those who feel valued learn for the teacher and win for the coach.[4] We also know from experience that church folks will stand in line to hear a good word from their respected and appreciative minister.

Some people question the appropriateness of positive reinforcement in ministry. "We should not try to motivate people by praising them. When we make encouragement a cornerstone of our way of doing ministry, we create a congregation of Pharisees, seeking credit for praying in the temple. You know what our Lord said of those folks. People are supposed to do what they do to the glory of God, not to receive a pat-on-the-back." Positive encouragement involves this risk. If large numbers of people succumb to the temptation, then the leader should make adjustments in procedures. Praise cannot be justified as a strategy to recruit followers. Nor should it be sought as the reward for becoming a follower.

However, Romans 12:8 identifies encouragement as a spiritual gift. Paul possessed it. He "confirmed the souls of the disciples" and "exhorted them to continue in the faith" (Acts 14:21-22). Peter, commissioned by Jesus to "strengthen" his brothers (Luke 22:32), encouraged the elders of the churches in their work (I Pet. 5:1-2).[5] Barnabas was called "The Son of Encouragement," not only because of the translation of his name but also because he bolstered the spirits of both Paul and Mark (Acts 4:36). Those who encourage others stand in line with some of the great leaders of the church.

This is not to say that a pastor can never be critical or offer negative comments. People will respond to criticism, complaints, and other forms of punishment. Negative reinforcement works, but it has two significant drawbacks. First, negative feedback, like an insecticide, must continually be increased to maintain its effectiveness. How unpleasant it would be to have to keep escalating criticism and complaints. This would make congregational life miserable.

Second, and more significantly, negative feedback tends to decrease undesirable behavior without increasing desirable behavior. Punishment may convince Billy to stop biting Johnny, but it does not necessarily follow that Billy will love Johnny. Public ridicule can keep folks from expressing racist opinions, but it does nothing to stop racism. In the church, we seek to change hearts as well as behaviors. Complaining, criticizing, and punishing are not as effective as appreciating, valuing, and rewarding.

Because It Is Sound Theology. The Christian faith helps people realize more of their potential. Through faith, otherwise immature, stumbling, inept, lazy human beings can do more and be more than they could ever hope to do or be without faith.[6]

A major component of this transformation comes when leaders bring people into contact with the teachings of the Gospel. Doing this encouragingly rather than discouragingly adds another powerful ingredient to the process of helping people realize more of their potential. As one of America's leading executives says, "An important skill is to be able to help people believe they can accomplish much more than they think they can."[7]

This transformation or realization happens in part because people tend to rise to the expectations of those whom they respect. When President Woodrow Wilson's secretary of labor died, one of the White House maids caught the president off guard with a request. "Mr. President, my husband runs a little store on Pennsylvania Avenue and really works hard. I wonder if you would consider making him Secretary of Labor?" Startled by her unexpected and rather unreasonable request, the President replied, "Well, Mary, that's a very critical position. It requires a big man." She replied, "Well, if you put my husband in that position, he'd be a big man."[8]

Although this story strains the limits of plausibility, this principle holds: people rise or fall according to expectation: levels. Church members nurtured on encouragement discover possibilities that would remain hidden if they heard only scorn and derision.

Dave Dungan leads the tenor section of his choir. The person who stands next to him says, "Dave pushes the outer limits of my singing ability. When he misses practice or Sunday worship, I struggle. His clear, beautiful voice charts a course my otherwise halting voice can follow. His gentle instruction and words of praise inspire me. Frankly, he gives me confidence in my ability. With his encouragement, I begin to realize my vocal potential."

The Gospel advocates this style of positive encouragement leadership. Jesus certainly ministered this way. He set people free to be the persons that God created them to be. The Master sought pro-active ways to improve people's mental, physical, and spiritual health. He sought to build relationships and to push people to realize their potential. Christian leadership should always follow his example.

Helpful Hints on Building a Positive Congregational Climate

The most fortunate clergy inherit congregations with positive climates for ministry and mission. The rest must intentionally plan and program to overcome the stale or even poisoned atmospheres. While this is seldom an easy task, some simple techniques are available.

Model Positive Behavior on Your Own Life and Ministry. More than any other person in the congregation, the minister sets the attitude thermostat. Erik Erickson told a story of a rabbi who felt inhibited when asked to make a speech in heaven. "I am good only at refutation," he said. Many clergy persons specialize in refutation. Using their keen insight, these pastors spot the errors in every program and the faults in every person. Other pastors spend most of their waking hours lamenting the universality of sin in the world at large and in their own congregations. Ministers who constantly complain, find fault, and see only the worst in others should not be surprised when the congregational atmosphere becomes poisoned.

Even when working at the task alone, the pastor improves the congregational climate considerably by emphasizing the positive while deemphasizing the negative. Pastor Toby uses both body and verbal language to build a more positive climate. Normally, he sits on the edge of his chair, looks the parishioner straight in the eye, smiles, and lovingly interrupts with comments such as, "Yes, yes, tell me about that." His manner conveys genuine care for the one to whom he speaks. If, however, the conversation turns to vicious gossip, frivolous complaint, or vague lamentation, he eases back in his chair, becomes passive, and stares at a distant spot on the wall. When the speaker turns the conversation in a positive direction or begins to focus on a significant issue of pastoral concern, Toby's attention returns. He slides forward in his chair and again participates in the conversation. Through speech and body language he has learned to discourage the negative and encourage the positive.

Frequently, without realizing it, we take for granted the good that people do while we constantly complain about the error of their ways. If we are not careful, we find ourselves complaining about our one problem in the midst of our two thousand blessings. To correct this, monitor the ratio between positives and negatives, complaints and compliments. Keep track of the ratio between errors detected and achievements celebrated. Whatever the results, commit yourself to increasing the positive side of the equation.

Keep in mind that even machines need more than repair. To function properly, machines must be monitored and regularly lubricated. They need preventive maintenance.

The abundant application of positive encouragement serves as the preventive maintenance of relationship building. The writer of Proverbs reminds us: "Kind words are like honey—sweet to the taste and good for your health" (Prov. 16:24 TEV). Not only does saying kind things strengthen us personally, but it also helps to keep the congregation functioning smoothly.

Build on Success. Sports figures argue convincingly that successes are built on success. Winners tend to continue winning. The momentum for motivation comes from having momentum. Bill Glass, once of the Cleveland Browns and now a Baptist minister, makes this point by insisting that winning teams have a high morale. Morale comes from winning. Winning engenders even higher morale. Obviously, if one wants to elevate a team's morale, one must help the team to claim a victory. Al McGuire, a former basketball coach and now a sports broadcaster, says that a good schedule will turn a good team into a great team. He suggests playing the opening game at home against "Cream Puff University." This ensures that the season starts with a winning record, which builds the confidence that the team will need later in the year for the tough games.

Even though the Christian faith is not a game and congregations differ significantly from teams, the same principle applies to both. Vital congregations have a high morale. This morale comes from doing things successfully. Further successes encourage higher morale.

Consequently, those seeking to change the climate of a low morale congregation should first plan for a few small victories. Do not advocate goals so high that failure might result. Low morale congregations know how to lose. They need to experience a victory—even a small one. When properly rooted in a spiritual focus, little successes raise morale sufficiently to enable the congregation to take on and later succeed at bigger challenges.

Jim Matthews describes how he applied the "winning leads to winning" principle to the church budget. "Our congregation used to have what we called a 'Faith Challenge Budget.' Each year, every ministry department developed a request for funding based on group brainstorming. 'If money were not an issue, what could we do next year?' was more of a factor than hard-headed budget planning.

"The stewardship department compiled all these requests and challenged the congregation to underwrite them with pledges. Obviously, the people's pledges never measured up to the committees' dreams. Each year the amount pledged was greater than the year before. There was not, however, any rejoicing. We always fell short of the committees' dreams because we had not achieved the goal. The congregation always believed themselves to be failures at stewardship.

"We finally changed that system. Now we have the financial drive *before* we write the budget. The pledges still increase about the same percentage from year to year, but we now can rejoice. Instead of feeling like failures, we feel successful. The stewardship division prepares a balanced budget based on what people pledge rather than what committees dream. Our people have always maintained their pledges. Now that we have a balanced budget, however, our financial reports make us appear successful. What a positive feeling that has brought to congregational life.

"The positive feelings we have about our stewardship spill into other areas of church life. Committees seem to do their ministries with more confidence. Since we don't have to interrupt the flow of the service with regular announcements about being behind in the budget, worship seems to be more congenial and spirited. Now that I don't have to worry about finances, I believe I even preach with more confidence. It is great."

Churches that have the right spiritual focus keep their expectations realistic and build on their successes by developing positive climates for ministry. In Jim's situation, the focus was shifted from the church's need to receive to the people's need to give.

Program to Make People Feel Valuable. Churches offer marriage enrichment weekends to help husbands and wives find ways to rekindle their abilities to make each other feel valuable.[9] Effective pastors develop programs that do this for the entire congregation. We want people to feel valuable. We want them to experience that very distinctive teaching of the Christian faith—"God believes you are very special!"

The ways to work toward this goal are limitless. The church newsletter can be used to mention significant accomplishments among the membership as well as to thank those who serve the church in special ways. Use Pentecost Sunday, the birthday of the Church, as *Honored Leaders Sunday.* Each year single out a few people who have given exceptional service to the church throughout their lifetimes. Engrave each of their names on a bronze plaque. Before the entire congregation, praise the service they have given. It leaves no doubt in the congregation's mind: "This church appreciates people."

Many wise pastors gear their personal ministries to appreciating others. Some set a monthly goal for writing thank-you notes to people in the church. One midwestern minister tries to write at least two clergy colleagues each month to tell them what a significant job he feels they do in their congregations.

One congregation holds a St. Florian Day Celebration in which they invite every firefighter in the community to be a special guest at a worship service during Fire Prevention Week. The same idea can be adapted for police, educators, health professionals, nursing home caregivers, and others. What tremendous community goodwill can be generated by saying, "What we do best is care."

V

LEADERS ARE ROLE MODELS

LEAD vb 1a: *to guide on a way, esp. by going in advance.*

Webster's New Collegiate Dictionary

The wise pastor accepts this burdensome reality: to be a leader one must be out in front to show the way. The minister's example significantly impacts the health and well-being of the church.

Members expect their pastors to exhibit the highest standards of Christian behavior. Sometimes these expectations are unbelievably high. Parishioners may even hold the minister to higher standards of conduct than they hold themselves or other church members. This kind of thinking often leads to the mistaken assumption that Christians would not know how to behave without the pastor's example. This makes the role of leadership exceedingly demanding!

Pastor, You're Not Just Any Other Person!

Larry has been pastor at Meadow Creek Church for nine years. His ministry there has been eventful. His wife left him for another man four years ago. When that happened, the people stood by him, not just because of sympathy but because they genuinely loved their pastor and had confidence in him.

Today Larry is embroiled in a controversy that threatens his continued ministry at Meadow Creek Church. As he explains, "One of those nosey parishioners saw my car parked overnight at my girl friend's house. That woman called the president of the congregation and complained. Now a petition is circulating that demands my resignation on the grounds of my 'immoral behavior.' Good grief, I am a forty-four-year-old single adult with grown children. My friend, Sue, and I have announced our forthcoming marriage. If I want to spend the night at her place, I will. We are consenting adults.

"The complaining is hypocritical. The church treasurer divorced his wife to marry the secretary with whom he had been having a relationship. People grumbled, but no one demanded *his* resignation. The woman who saw my car at Sue's house is one of the most vicious gossips west of the Mississippi River. The church tolerates her. Why should a different standard be applied to the minister than to the members?"

Larry's rhetorical query describes the reality of a minister's life. More than other public figures, clergy persons serve as role models. Professional athletes and teachers were once expected to be moral examples. This is no longer necessarily true. Professional athletes consider themselves to be wealthy entertainers, not examples of moral rectitude or hero models for children. Relaxed community standards and a flood of litigation have determined that public school teachers should be considered ordinary folks. Politicians, on the other hand, have probably never been considered to have high standards of behavior. Over and over again, the voting public demonstrates that anything except murder and mayhem is acceptable in government—as long as the constituency feels reasonably well-served and private interest groups get special consideration.

Congregations, however, expect more of their ministers

than they do of teachers, politicians, or athletes. One seldom, if ever, hears a congregation say of their pastor, "Well, he lies, cheats, and steals. You cannot trust him with a confidence. He drinks to excess, has several 'girl friends' other than his wife, and never pays his bills. However, no one has ever kept our membership records as neatly and accurately as he. Therefore, we have asked the district superintendent to let him stay for another five years!"

While people might say something comparable of a legislator, educator, or athlete, they expect the minister to maintain a higher standard of conduct. The pastor's human frailties or fairness to his or her family may not be taken into consideration. A congregation wants the pastor to set a good example. Church members almost always assume and demand congruity between the minister's behavior and the congregation's definition of Christian behavior.

This high expectation has biblical precedence. A pastoral letter instructs Tit. "to appoint church elders in every town. Remember my instructions: an elder must be without fault." The writer goes on to remind the Church of specific details, including marital fidelity and the need for well-behaved children, before explaining that this criteria must be maintained because ". . . he is in charge of God's Work" (1:5-7 TEV).

Thomas Oden traces this topic through the Bible and patristic writings before observing that the Early Church had a seemingly deliberate list of four preliminary qualifications for what became the office of ordained ministry: (1) unimpeachable character, (2) sexual fidelity in marriage, (3) being a good parent, and (4) "under no imputation of loose living."[1]

Of these qualifications, good parenting surprises us. It holds that the elder's children should not only be believers but also should not have the "reputation of being wild or disobedient" (Tit. 1:6 TEV). We might ask an obvious question: Why did the Church consider this an essential quality for leaders?

Although it is impossible to know for certain, we can conjecture that this qualification may compare to the request for references on a job application. Perhaps the ancients wanted to know, "Do you have a leadership track record? Have you been able to impact lives? Do your own children pay attention to you?" The other qualifications state that ministers must have a higher standard of conduct. People expect the pastor to pay bills, obey leash laws, make every effort to parent responsibly, take a bath regularly, and dress appropriately. In addition, the leader must discipline sexual urges—both to avoid gossip and to conserve life's creative energy for ministry rather than self-indulgence. After all, the behavior of the church's leader reflects the Christian ministry of the faith community. This seems to be the assumption underlying these four qualifications. Whether we like it or not, the minister's behavior is perceived to speak for the church.

Note the Added Burden: Ministers Speak for the Church. When Ron graduated from seminary, he came to Cloverlawn to serve as rector of St. Luke's. Both his seminary and his mother had drilled him on the importance of public appearance and decent conduct. No one, however, informed him that when he spoke, others heard St. Luke's Church.

Ron considered himself particularly well-prepared to serve the prophetic role. Imagine his disappointment when he discovered that the social ills of this little community of 6,000 inhabitants were not nearly as glaring as they had been in Chicago, where he attended seminary. Cloverlawn had no homeless people. Public housing was modest but adequate. The nearly homogeneous population minimized racial conflict.

Instead of becoming involved in significant social issues, Ron found himself relegated to writing letters to the editor of the local newspaper. Hardly a week passed that his name did not appear on the editorial page—chastising, correcting, or cajoling someone in the city for something. He expressed himself publicly on every community controversy. Once, he even found it necessary to pontificate on how the Johnson Road sewer should pass down the west side of the street instead of the east side.

The inevitable controversy that ensued at St. Luke's took several months to sort out. Eventually, Ron came to understand that his propensity to say something about everything troubled his congregation. The people agreed that he was permitted to have and to express an opinion. He could never, however, be considered just another Cloverlawn citizen. Because he pastored St. Luke's, others considered his pronouncements to be either the policy of the local congregation or the faithful expression of the Church. With the office of ordained ministry comes a burden of responsibility. As John Gardner says, "Leaders are symbols. They seldom speak for themselves."

Leaders Teach by Example

Modeling desirable behavior gets results. Television executives understand this. Twenty years ago almost everyone seen on television smoked. No one was shown fastening a seatbelt. Only the town drunk demonstrated the effects of drinking alcohol, and on the "Andy Griffith Show" he was loveable and humorous.

Today, seldom does an actor or actress light a cigarette on television. Only the most irresponsible characters fail to buckle up. When alcohol is served at parties on television shows, a designated driver sometimes is appointed. Although far from being consistently socially responsible, television has caught on to the importance of modeling desirable behavior.

Widely recognized public figures as well as persons in positions of authority and responsibility train others by their actions and inactions. Sometimes people follow an example because they want to please their leader. At other times, they find their leader's example convincing. Whatever the reason, keep this in mind: examples are powerful.[2]

Expecting leaders to set the example is a scriptural mandate. I Peter exhorts elders to "tend the flock of God that is your charge." Then the writer directs that this be done "not as domineering over those in your charge but by being examples to the flock" (5:2-3). Paul, never one to hesitate about putting himself on the front line, urged the Christians in Corinth to "be imitators of me, as I am of Christ" (I Cor. 11:1). When he wrote the Philippians, he again recommended his example: "Join with others in following my example, brothers, and take note of those who live according to the pattern we gave you" (3:17 NIV).

Ministers still teach by modeling Christian behavior. Our example will not, of course, be perfect. We will struggle and stumble. On those difficult occasions, our example must be one of seeking to repent, needing to be forgiven, and searching for God's healing wholeness. A congregation may find this example most beneficial when offered in the midst of a troubled moment.

Paul stressed the importance of modeling a Christian life-style, because so few examples existed in the pagan world of his day. Not much has changed. Modern pastors still set an example for those who might not otherwise recognize Christian behavior. After all, if leaders do not model the faith, then who will? And if no one does, how will an understanding of Christian conduct be passed from generation to generation?

It might be argued that the ranks of Christian examples have thinned significantly in this often-called post-church era. The money and sex scandals among the American media's high visibility religious leaders, the television evangelists, underscores the shortcomings of the recent revival sweeping the country which places more emphasis on feeling religious than on moral conduct. As the level of biblical illiteracy grows, the sources of information on Christian behavior diminish. Quite frankly, only a paucity of positive examples exists.

A historic strength of mainline Protestantism has been openness. We have insisted that the truth of what God has done in Jesus Christ cannot be circumscribed by one creed, sect, opinion, or perspective. Unfortunately, this openness to truth has led many to wrongly conclude that mainline churches teach that it doesn't matter what you believe. Some clergy persons compound the difficulty by trying to convince the unchurched that "since religious people are just like everyone else, you should join us."

We will not motivate many by offering a faith that anticipates no change in beliefs or behavior for one's life. The present age yearns for clear articulations of the Christian faith modeled in the daily lives of those who claim to believe. They cry out "Show me the difference that faith makes!"

If those called to positions of leadership do not serve as role models, then who will? Where else can this biblically illiterate generation turn for illustrations?

A Complication: Style Frequently Ranks Higher Than Competence. "I cannot understand it," Marvin, pastor of Belgrade Road Church, lamented. "I am the best preacher this congregation has had since Dr. MacArthur retired in 1938. The Christian education program, which I implemented, has been acclaimed for excellence in two professional journals. I updated the membership records, which had not been touched for decades. My skills in programming, preaching, and administration are outstanding. Yet the members of this church don't appreciate me. They do nothing but complain. Granted, I do get a little grumpy with the old ladies' Sunday school class. And, I admit, I told off that old curmudgeon, Joe Smith, at the hardware store. All right, so my fuse is a little short. That doesn't change the fact that I am a very competent minister!"

Marvin has stumbled upon an irony of pastoral ministry. Congregations rank ministerial style and personality higher than competence. Marvin may be skilled, but the congregation experiences him as cantankerous and impatient—not gifted. The members of Belgrade Road Church also describe him as being bullheaded about making decisions, loose-lipped with confidences, judgmental about his detractors, flippant toward those he considers unimportant, and perhaps most distressing to the membership, uncaring about the widows' Sunday school class.

Issues of style and personality take precedence over competence in business and government as well as congregational life. Andrew Sherwood, a well-known human resource consultant, lists the characteristics that distinguish good leaders from great leaders. These traits speak more to matters of style than skill. They include the courage to make decisions, the willpower to carry through, the flexibility to adapt to change, the demonstrated yearning to learn, and the lived-out commitment to honesty and the values people admire and respect. In other words, great leaders have personal integrity.[3]

A recent poll suggests that people vote for personality before competence even when choosing a president. The question of who will be elected president seems to be related to three areas: (1) personality, (2) stands on the issues, and (3) political affiliation. The poll concluded that our most recent presidents have been elected primarily on the basis of personality rather than issues or party affiliations.

The participants involved in a consultation on renewing mainline flagship congregations were asked to list characteristics they felt would be desired in pastoral leadership for the 1980s and beyond.[4] These suggestions fell under two headings: attitudes and abilities. Among the seventeen attitudes were flexibility, a sense of humor, optimism, a trust of people, ego security, a biblically oriented vision, and personal stamina. The list of eighteen abilities included skills in preaching, conflict management, administration, and delegation.

The study noted that these ideal attitudes and abilities sometimes appear to be mutually exclusive. Leaders must be flexible but still have a disciplined sense of direction. Their style should embody both urgency and patience. Leaders must accept people where they are *and* offer a vision of where they should go. While the servant role best fits pastoral leadership, ministers must also be comfortable enough with power to delegate responsibilities with authority. When contemplated carefully, the role of pastor as leader overwhelms. The task demands that one be all things to all people under all circumstances—even when this requires displaying opposite qualities simultaneously. No wonder every congregation which is asked "What do you want in a new minister?" compiles a list of criteria describing Jesus, Paul, Peter, and Andrew!

Rather than disregarding these paradoxical expectations as impossible to fulfill, they should be viewed as mutually fulfilling facets of ministry. Accepting people where they are does not preclude affirming their possibilities. Leaders can urge people and still be patient with them. A minister can have power and delegate responsibility and still be a servant. In fact, Peter may be instructing church leaders about how to handle this when he says, "Don't be a tyrant, but lead by your good example" (I Pet. 5:3 TLB).

Effective leadership frequently rests on whether or not the congregation perceives a mutual "liking" and respect between minister and people. Pastors who are unconcerned for the health and well-being of the congregation seldom offer heroic examples of leadership. Congregations that do not approve of their pastors seldom offer them even the possibility of leadership. Accepting and loving one another constitutes the bottom line of Christianity. When we try to make people feel loved and appreciated by serving them, we model our faith.

The High Price of Leadership

Although salvation is free, everything else costs something. Keep this in mind when calculating the cost of being a pastoral minister. Leadership has a very high price. Ministers are held to a higher standard of conduct than the members of their congregations. They are expected to be role models of faithful living to the community. Yet people evaluate them according to "likeableness" more than competence. What a burden to carry!

In order to carry the load, pastors need a strong calling. Jesus says, "You did not choose me, I chose you" (John 15:16). The minister who disagrees by believing himself or herself to be more of a volunteer than a conscript will not be able to handle the stress. God's call to leadership has never promised a pain-free, stress-free life. From Abraham to Moses to Peter to Paul to the present generation, God's call to ministry has demanded a great deal from those who responded.

Ironically, that which requires so much energy, loving those we are called to serve, restores our strength. Loving others benefits the one who offers the love. Ministers experience this when we hear others quote passages from our sermons that have strengthened them through hard times, when we receive letters of appreciation from people we have assisted, or when we watch the joy of families we have counseled. A servant to God's people can be energized by serving.

For this reason, we need not view serving others and desiring approval as constant negatives. Personal benefits accrue. The performance of ministerial responsibilities contributes to personal development. Leadership could never be sustained without a strong sense of self-worth. Loving one's neighbor as oneself both requires and contributes to a healthy self-love. Self-esteem grows from selfless service. Jesus stated this principle. "You will know them by their fruits" (Matt. 7:16). The more we offer loving service, the more likely we are to be approved and thereby enhance our self-esteem. By loving neighbor as self and being a faithful servant to the family of God, the minister finds the strength to be the role model that he or she is called to be.

————— VI —————

LEADERS EXPECT EXCELLENCE

Brooks become crooked
from taking the path
of least resistance.
So do people.

"*Crookedness*" *Harold Kohn*

For many years Admiral Hyman Rickover headed the United States Nuclear Navy. Although admirers and critics held opposing views about his stern and demanding personality, few doubted his capacity to lead. The Admiral customarily interviewed every officer aboard a nuclear submarine. These sessions frequently left the interviewees emotionally spent.

Former President Jimmy Carter once applied for service under Rickover. They began a grueling two-hour conversation in which the young Carter chose the discussion topics. Eventually, the Admiral asked Carter how well he had performed at the Naval Academy. The yet-to-be-President Carter responded proudly. He had graduated fifty-ninth in a class of 820. The Admiral responded by asking, "Did you do your best?" Before he could get an affirmative answer across his lips, Mr. Carter recalled several times when he failed to perform to the best of his ability. He candidly said, "No, sir, I did not always do my best." After a long and painful pause, the Admiral concluded the interview with "Why not?"[1] That encounter became the formative idea for Carter's book *Why Not the Best?* The same idea should also challenge every man and woman called to ministry. Like undisciplined streams, when people take the path of least resistance, their lives become gnarled and twisted. Perfection dwells beyond the possible, but we who claim to walk with Christ are called to give the very best we have in service to the Creator.

In every field of endeavor, effective leaders never content themselves with the average. They strive for excellence. Expecting the best from self and others often requires swimming upstream. Our society not only tolerates mediocrity, but it seems to have also made it our performance standard.[2] Who among us has not pondered whether the term *service station* now qualifies as an oxymoron? Has not "Buy American" become an appeal to loyalty rather than an advertisement for the highest quality?

J. Irwin Miller, business and church leader, reminds us that it is expensive to be mediocre. Even more than lack of money, failing to strive for the best depletes confidence and self-esteem. Accepting the mediocre gives us a year-long "New Year's Day Hangover"—not well enough to go jogging but not sick enough to die.

Although it is unfair to say that the Church sets mediocrity as the standard, mediocrity is frequently the perceived standard. For more than two decades, mainline Protestantism has been declining in number of members and influence. Too often we merely cite the enormously complex sociological reasons for this occurrence. Many people are even content to accept the eventual and inevitable demise of these great churches.

When we have this attitude, we are evading responsibility for those circumstances under our control. For example, part of the decline can be traced to the working assumption that evangelism takes care of itself, and thus we need neither make plans nor give effort to accomplish church growth. Past generations made "church planting" a priority. We behave almost as though new congregations spring from the soil as spontaneously as weeds. Consequently, the formation of new, intentional congregations has not kept pace with moving populations, nor have capital funding programs been in place to enable the formation of these congregations.

Furthermore, we seem to have assumed that the next generation will automatically take its turn in the pew. This has not happened. The average age among mainline Protestants approaches that of the United States Senate simply because we are failing to communicate the importance of church attendance to our own children. Contrary to popular opinion, conservative churches are not draining membership from mainline churches. Most of those who once formed the mainline constituency simply stay home on Sunday morning. The real problem is this: Local pastors and denominational executives alike have failed to maintain high standards for the ministry of congregations.

Joe Smith is an exemplary picture of mediocrity at work in personal ministry. He has the remarkable ability to consistently go through the motions without getting results. His worship services bear the unmistakable mark of having been thrown together. No one seems to have trouble refusing his requests to help at the fellowship dinner. He can follow every step in the "Every Member Canvas" manual, but the campaign fails miserably. He does not demand the best of himself or of his parishioners. In fact, he does not even do enough to get by. His goal? To say, "Well, I did everything I could do. It is not my fault." Rather than laissez-faire, his style can be classified as fairly lazy. Unfortunately, such mediocrity has become widespread.

Leaders and the Passion for Excellence

Australian football coach Ron Barassi distinguishes the professional from the amateur by noting, "A professional is dedicated to the eradication of error. It has nothing to do with money."[3] Certainly the work of the church professional should not be undertaken with less resolve than this! The ordained minister should strive for nothing less than the best worship, nurture, pastoral care, mission, administration, and all other functions of ministry.

Sir Thomas Beecham did not relish guest conducting. When the musicians did not know him and the rehearsal time was limited, the results were often less than outstanding. After a particularly difficult evening as guest conductor, Sir Thomas had dinner with friends. One friend inquired what the orchestra had played. "I don't know what they *played*," Sir Thomas admitted, "but I *conducted* Mozart."

A minister should have the same high standards. Prepare every sermon as if it were to be delivered on Easter Sunday. Teach every lesson as if Paul were sitting in the class waiting to critique you. Make every pastoral visit believing that God will use you to push the button of hope for someone whose life has hit bottom.

Even doing a *little* better can have amazing results. Some years ago, Jack Nicklaus topped PGA money-winners. He earned more than three times as much as Arnold Palmer, the runner-up. That whopping fiscal difference resulted from an average of only 1½ fewer strokes per game! Nicklaus averaged 69.81 strokes per game and Palmer averaged 71.30.

Slight improvements make a profound difference in the local church as well. Those who usually—but not always—do their best need to be reminded that wondrous things result from slightly elevated goals in stewardship and evangelism, from spending a little more time in prayer and study, and from giving a little more polish to the homilies.

Effective leaders never conclude the week without pondering, "Have I done my best?" Those who answer affirmatively experience deep satisfaction in ministry.

Leaders Also Expect the Best from Others

Abraham Lincoln and a friend attended a church service one Sunday morning. Afterwards, the friend commented on the minister's fine sermon. Lincoln disagreed with that assessment. "I didn't think it was very good," the president commented. "But why?" the friend queried. "It is simple," said Mr. Lincoln, "he didn't ask us to do anything great." Effective leaders not only demand excellence of themselves, but they also expect the same of those they lead. If we do not expect greatness, then we surely will not get it.

In everything it does, the Church witnesses to its faith. For this reason, nothing slipshod or haphazard can be tolerated. Pastoral leaders should be well prepared for every meeting and should expect the same from others. Within the limits of responsible stewardship and financial possibility, the church building must be properly cleaned and maintained. High standards must be set for Sunday school teachers, Bible study leaders, and worship leaders. The membership must be challenged by the call for excellence in stewardship, mission, and ministry. High performance comes from high performance standards. After all, we do these things in service to God. We cannot offer or expect anything less than the best.

Exotic fish stores report that sharks have become a popular aquarium fish. If sharks are caught and confined when small, they grow only to a size proportionate to the aquarium. The limited environment determines their growth. Sharks can be six inches long and still be fully matured. Only when set free in the ocean do they grow to their normal length of eight feet.[4] Environment also helps to determine the emotional and spiritual sizes to which people grow. When people are offered greater possibilities, challenges, and expectations, they are more likely to soar (within reasonable limits). Leaders understand this. They prod, probe, and push followers to higher levels.

Our faith promises the possibility of a more deeply satisfying life. Consequently, church leaders want people to have better marriages, to be more attentive parents, to be more committed to spiritual growth, and to strive more ardently for the coming Kingdom. Effective leaders communicate these expectations and related programs in ways to make fulfillment possible.

Leaders Have an Eye for a Better Way

In 1910, a devoted church member bequeathed the Springtown Church five acres of fertile farmland. The benefactor wanted the church to use the land for any form of ministry. Originally, the congregation planned to build a parsonage. Until funds could be raised, they decided to plant corn on the vacant land.

For nearly three-quarters of a century, the farmers of the Springtown congregation took turns planting and harvesting. Each spring and fall they argued about whose turn it was to care for the little plot of land at the edge of town. John, their seminary student minister, realized that funds that had not been raised in two generations would probably never be raised. He could not help but notice as well that the debates over plowing, planting, and harvesting became more rancorous each year. Therefore, he sought an alternative solution. He suggested that the land be used for a community park. This satisfied the benefactor's intent and spread responsibility among more people. The entire community could help maintain a park. Only those with farm machinery could plant and harvest. Within a matter of months, children played on the same land that had divided the congregation.

John demonstrated leadership insight. He proposed a new solution to an old problem. Leaders either have this ability or they rely on the counsel of those who do. An eye for a better way makes it possible to see answers as well as questions, to distinguish good ideas from bad ones, to offer solutions that work instead of proposals that compound problems.

This eye for a good idea includes the capacity for innovation. For twelve hundred years after the domestication of the horse, people rode bareback. The Chinese introduced the saddle and improved the ride significantly. Two centuries later the Chinese added stirrups. Moveable footstraps allowed the rider greater personal freedom as well as control over the horse. This innovation made riding horses in combat possible. Consequently, military historians regard the stirrup as the most significant invention prior to gun powder. The Han Dynasty soldier who suggested the stirrup had the capacity to see a new possibility in an old idea. Today we call such people *innovators*. Their gift of innovation is crucial to the leadership task.

Although someone occasionally stumbles upon the monumentally new, most innovations result from reworking old ways of thinking and doing. The minister's contribution to the renewal of worship might be a radically new way of praising God. More likely, however, the innovative minister sees what others fail to notice. A congregation's worship frequently can be transformed by urging the organist to stop dragging the hymns and by asking the speakers to eliminate "dead time" by moving with dispatch from chair to lectern to pulpit. Simple suggestions often have profound consequences. Ecclesiastical innovators can do for church life what the Han Dynasty soldier did for horseback riding.

Beware of the power of a new idea to take an unexpected, positive, productive direction. In 1943, the president of a company which manufactured typewriters and adding machines speculated, "I think there's a world market for about five computers." Some local church leader probably had similar thoughts about using mass telephoning to start new congregations, televising local worship services, and organizing congregations of different denominations into ecumenical councils for ministry and mission.

A minister might be as surprised as that business machine president at the success of an idea. On the other hand, almost nothing new works perfectly in its first trial or model. Innovation always involves risk. We risk failure each time we introduce a new idea. If the idea works even a little, then changes must be implemented which in turn may cause new problems.[5]

A leader must accept that risk opens new opportunities for failure. John Wooden, one of the most successful coaches in college basketball history, claimed that the willingness to risk making errors is key to winning. *Doers* learn from making mistakes. This truth applies to businesses, governments, and churches as well as team sports.[6]

We often try to encourage one another by saying that we must learn from our mistakes. Regrettably, some are not willing to reflect long enough on their mistakes to make this possible. It is said of one well-traveled clergy person, "He does not have forty years experience in ministry. He has two years' experience repeated twenty times!" Learn from your mistakes.

Avoid the Pit of Perfectionism

Do your best! God asks nothing more of us, and we should ask nothing less of ourselves. Likewise, a competent leader never asks for less than the best from others.

This expectation for excellence, however, must be held in tension with the fact that others will disappoint us regularly. Others will not always give their all. Nor do ministers always excel. We are sinners doing ministry in a sinful world with other sinful people. We will not attain personal perfection nor eradicate error from others. Those whose expectation for excellence becomes a compulsion for perfection go the way of the shooting star. They burn out before touching the horizon. Effective leaders expect excellence but know that they must settle for less than perfection. Fortunately, by faith we can settle for less. "Such is the confidence that we have through Christ toward God. Not that we are sufficient of ourselves to claim anything as coming from us; our sufficiency is from God, who has qualified us to be ministers of a new covenant" (II Cor. 3:4-6).

What a sustaining faith we proclaim. God asks for our best—nothing more, nothing less. When our best fails, as it will from time to time, we grow from the experience. Faith assures us that nothing, not even failure, separates us from the love of God. Knowing this makes risking our best worthwhile.

VII

LEADERS WORK HARD

It takes all the running you can do to keep in the same place. If you want to get somewhere else, you must run at least twice as fast.

Lewis Carroll, Alice in Wonderland

This advice given to Alice in her new and strange world applies to the pastor working with a local congregation. Ministerial leadership requires natural ability, learned skills, and twice the effort it takes to stand still.

One pastor says that he does not feel settled in a new office until he arranges his diplomas on the wall. "I used to think these indicators of formal training certified me for ministry," he says. "Now I realize that, at best, they only quiet my anxiety in a new and strange environment." A master of divinity, even iced with a doctorate of ministry, does not make one a pastoral leader.

Just as one does not become a carpenter without having firsthand experience with nails, wood, and tools, so one does not become a pastoral leader without properly rooted motivations and firsthand knowledge of individuals and congregations. Experience empowers the assorted tools one gains from education. For this to happen, one must be willing to invest an enormous amount of time and energy. No sluggard need aspire to church leadership. According to the writer of Proverbs, "laziness ends in slave labor" (12:24*b* NIV). Becoming a leader is more like building a suspension bridge than growing an oak tree. An acorn does not choose risks nor devise personal strategies. It becomes a tree quite naturally. As long as an acorn receives proper sunlight, soil, and rain and avoids being eaten by a squirrel, its genetic code determines what it becomes. Leaders, on the other hand, like bridges, are built intentionally. They are assembled one piece at a time—often under dangerous and demanding circumstances.

For this reason, clergy persons cannot be content to go through life getting lifts from others and waiting until actions are forced upon them. Even the most talented can fizzle if they permit laziness to undermine their ministries. God's gifts always come as raw materials. They must be shaped, polished, and diligently maintained. This takes hard work. The effective pastor hears and responds affirmatively to the message of Koheleth, "Whatever your hand finds to do, do it with all your might" (Eccles. 9:10 NIV). Without commitment to hard work, the job simply will not be done. Natural gifts must be accompanied by a willingness to spend sufficient time and energy on achieving effectiveness and competence.

Those of limited talent frequently excel in ministry by compensating for their lack of natural gifts with an overabundance of commitment. With sufficient investment of time and effort, they become better preachers. They cover for a less than brilliant intellect with grim determination. They struggle to become better organized. Lessons that others know instinctively they gain by trial and error.

To test this assertion, make a list of pastors considered to be outstanding leaders by their colleagues. Study their ministries carefully. Talk with them about what they do, how they do it, and how they have learned. The majority will be moderately talented but hard working people who are driven by a deep commitment to ministry. A surprising number will be undertalented overachievers. Only rarely will one stumble upon an effective pastoral leader who expends very little time or energy in ministry. His or her incredibly high level of talent negates the need for hard work.

It is said that the most successful business executives work, on average, fifty-seven hours per week. The best business-men realize that doing an excellent job requires more than the minimum time investment. In fact, the most effective govern their office schedules on the FILO principle—first in, last out. Corporate CEO and church pastor share this principle: Hard work can overcome many deficiencies.

The most effective equation for outstanding leadership is extraordinary gifts plus a good education empowered by practical experience and applied with boundless energy. To paraphrase the somewhat cynical aphorism of Damon Runyon: "It may be that the race is not always to the swift, success not always to the one who works the hardest, nor the battle to the strongest—but that's the way to bet."

Work Hard and Work Smart

At the close of the Second World War, my father joined the exodus from the city to the country. He bought an acre of land on a rural road and made plans to erect his dream house. Even without prior experience, he knew the basement must come first. He paid a teenage neighbor $1 per hour to help him. The two spent evenings and weekends for an entire summer digging the basement with hand shovels. It was exhausting, but my father was young and energetic. The neighbor boy was thrilled to have the job.

The truck driver who delivered the cement blocks for the foundation taught my father something important. An excavating company could have dug the basement with a mechanical shovel in one day. Not only would this have been easier and faster, but it also would have been more economical. A bulldozer would have cost less than my father paid the teenager to help dig it by hand!

Ministers, like home builders, soon learn that hard work

will not suffice. One must also work smart. Most ministers can find enough to keep busy nine days each week, twenty-seven hours each day. The enormity of the task necessitates learning a few tricks of the trade. Tex Sample relates the experience of being the visiting baseball team in Bogue Chitto, Mississippi. The opponent's field fell short of regulation. Left field contained a stand of pine trees in fair territory. Whenever one of the hometown boys dropped one into those pines, the visitors never seemed to be able to locate the ball before the fellow circled the bases. When a visiting player hit one into the pines, the locals always seemed to be able to run into the woods and come out immediately with the ball. As Sample puts it, "What were homeruns for them were only long singles for us." What appeared as remarkable skill was later explained by the discovery that the home team kept a sack of baseballs hidden behind a tree in the woods.[1]

Church leaders cannot resort to cheating. On the other hand, one can learn principles for ministry and management that function similarly to the sack of well-placed baseballs. Here are five such principles:

1. Keep Your Priorities Straight. "What do you have to do today?" Pastor Bob's wife asked as he headed out the parsonage door toward the church.

"I have nothing on the schedule. I will just sit at my desk while I wait for the phone to ring and the people to stop by. I'm sure the day will fill quickly," he cheerfully shouted over his shoulder.

Typically, a pastor need not plan the day's schedule. Interruption will fill each day beyond capacity. Busyness, however, does not constitute effectiveness. One must plan for interruptions without letting "what happens to come up" determine the agenda for ministry. Leaders must set priorities and goals that are pursued with the determination of a St. Bernard through a snowstorm.

Lee Iaccoca heads the Chrysler Corporation, one of America's largest corporations. In spite of working in an extremely complex and competitive industry, he insists on keeping his priorities written on a single sheet of paper. The local church pastor does not need a full sheet of paper. On a three-by-five-inch card, write down the most important things you are trying to do. What are your priorities? What business are you in? At least once a day, read that card. Those who don't have a clear focus on priorities dissipate their energies trying to do too many things for too many people in too many different directions.

Unlike many professions, ministry has no natural boundaries. Almost any activity can be considered ministry. For this reason, clergy must constantly discipline themselves to maintain excellence in the primary functions of ministry. James Glasse refers to this as "paying the rent." He reminds ministers that most parishes set requirements for their pastors. The fact that these requirements are not written on paper does not negate their importance. They are imprinted in the memory banks of every member. The minister must provide three things: (1) Preaching and worship: Sunday morning must be "done" well. (2) Teaching and pastoral care: The people must know that the minister cares for them. The minister must also teach children and intellectually stimulate adults. (3) Organization and administration: The parish has a right to expect sufficient organizational leadership to enable the congregation to do mission and ministry. The minister can engage in other forms of ministry after "paying the rent," but these things must be done extremely well.[2]

Never stray from effective preaching, teaching, administrating, caring, visioning, and so forth. These are to pastoral ministry what hitting, pitching, and fielding are to baseball. Do them well and be amazed at how smoothly everything else goes. On the other hand, the pastor without clear priorities, without a succinct personal mission statement, without clearly articulated goals, or without attentiveness to the fundamentals risks failure.

Always remember that jobs accumulate. Life is crammed full of important stuff. People regularly ask ministers to get involved, and parsons tend to respond positively. Over a period of time, responsibilities grow beyond the worthwhile to the burdensome. Review your calendar at least annually. Revise your schedule. Limit interruptions. Delete activities that others can do. Make certain that ample time and energy are given to preaching, teaching, caring, and administrating. Effective time management liberates one from the drudgery of overabundant busyness.

2. Know Your Limits. Jane McMurray admits her shortcomings: "My associate meets with the Christian education committee. I am not very creative in educational matters. I don't do children's sermons unless I absolutely cannot find someone else. It takes me longer to prepare a five-minute talk for children than a twenty-minute sermon for adults. I am a good counselor, but I refer the deeply troubled. The needs of many people go beyond my training and time limits."

One cannot be all things to all people under all conditions. That capacity extends beyond the range of human capability. Experienced pastors not only accept this as truth but they do not even try to be and do all things. Wise leaders run with their strengths and recruit others to cover their weaknesses.

3. Learn to Say No Graciously. The minister who does not know how to decline a request without offending the requester will not have long, congenial, effective pastorates. Those who respond positively to everything may suffer frequent bouts with nervous exhaustion. Those who regularly irritate people by refusing to comply with requests will likely relocate biannually.

Learn to ask permission to refuse. "May I say no to your request? If I agree to do this for you, it will be necessary for me to leave my family on the only free night I have that week." Another option: "If I accept your kind invitation, I will not be able to devote the necessary time to another equally important project that I have already accepted." Work closely with the church committee responsible for the pastor-parish relationship. Say, "Yes, that's a worthy idea.

But I'll need your help to decide what to give up in order to spend the necessary time on this additional role."

4. Save Everything You Write. Ministers preach, pray, and teach regularly. Each presentation requires special preparation. By carefully preserving and then reworking one's creative efforts, the material for one setting can frequently be recycled. The study one does for sermons can serve as material for a Bible study and vice-versa. Not only can sermons be rewritten several years later but they also can be reworked into talks for small church groups. Two-year-old sermon illustrations can worm their way into the pastor's article in the weekly newsletter. Form letters and invocations can always be reworked and reused.

5. Know the Congregation Well. A pastor helped sponsor a youth work trip to Mexico. The journey required taking a train from the capital city to the distant village where their missionary hosts would meet them. As the train pulled away from the station, the porter oriented the youth group for the journey. Limited familiarity with each other's native tongue compounded by the porter's heavy accent on the few English words he spoke created difficulties in communication.

At one point, the porter attempted to explain the significance of two doors in the railroad car. He believed those doors to be incredibly important for the journey. Did one open a passage to safety? Did the other house the fire extinguisher? The members of the group did not understand why he insisted on explaining these doors. He grew more and more impatient. His gestures became more vigorous, and his voice grew louder. After several frustrating minutes, the group realized that he was identifying the bathrooms.

Later in the trip, the group burst into laughter after one of the girls returned from the restroom. The railroad car was manufactured in the United States. Above each door, in English were the words *Men* and *Women*. Their thoughtful porter was more zealous than effective. He had not stopped to think about things from their perspective.

Although this lack of association is both understandable and acceptable for Mexican Pullman porters who are orienting foreign visitors, pastors cannot survive without a thorough understanding of the congregations that they lead. The minister must speak the language of the membership, be comfortable with its way of thinking, and understand its values. Be steeped in the cultural nuances of the people. Know the basic political orientation of the community. Learn the history of both the church and the area. A thorough understanding of a congregation's thinking and doing does not make the job easy, but it does keep the job within the limits of possibility.

The Blessedness of Good Fortune

It never hurts to be lucky. When attempting to economize on effort, being lucky can be as beneficial as working smart. Remember that Sir Alexander Fleming discovered penicillin when a speck of dust happened to land on an uncovered culture plate. Charles Goodyear discovered how to make rubber more durable when he accidentally dropped a beaker of sulphur into his experiment. These fellows understood the blessedness of good fortune.

Ministry offers comparable stories. Glen pastors one of the fastest growing congregations in his denomination. He was asked to reveal the secret of the remarkable growth of his congregation to a national gathering of clergy. He candidly told them, "Our building is located on one of the busiest streets in the fastest growing suburb of the fastest growing city in America. Three different denominations can report their most rapidly growing congregations within two miles of our location."

Other pastors must credit sheer good luck for the successes they enjoy. Some people lead charmed lives. A congregation's record of stewardship excels because the members happen to be both wealthy and generous. Another has an outstanding adult choir because a very gifted person volunteered to direct. Still another happened to be given the opportunity to work with a congregation filled with exceptionally committed lay leaders.

Good luck helps. It does not, however, replace hard work and competence. Other congregations near Glen's church have never grown. Their pastors have not invested sufficient effort to energize the location's possibilities. The poor stewardship habits of many wealthy people have never been challenged. Some congregations never utilize the talents of their best lay leaders. In Matthew 25, Jesus told a story about three servants entrusted with varying amounts of money. In the end, each was blessed or cursed, not according to what he had received, but according to whether or not he had made the best of the circumstances.

Good fortune, like all God's gifts, comes as raw material. One must act intentionally to take advantage of it. In fact, exceptional effort can be mistaken for luck. Alexander Fleming's and Charles Goodyear's good fortune came in the midst of many years of effort. The same can be said of many effective pastoral leaders. While good luck helps, we sometimes mistake Dame Fortune for hard work. As newspaper columnist Bob Talbert aptly states, "If you observe people long enough, you'll realize that the self-made ones have an abundance of working parts."

It Never Hurts to Love the Work

One summer evening, Thomas Edison returned home late from his laboratory. His wife pleaded with him, "You have been working too long without a rest. You must take a vacation." "But where will I go?" he asked. "Decide where you would rather be than anywhere on earth and go there," she told him. "Very well, that is what I will do," her husband responded. Early the next morning, Edison returned to his laboratory!

Rather than dismiss him as a workaholic, we might better understand Edison as a person who loved his work. That lab wore him out, but since he found such satisfaction in being there, it also energized him. The local church can do the same for the leader who loves what he or she does. Being a minister means living in a fish bowl—where at least 10 percent of the fish are piranha. Each task and every relationship takes its pound of flesh. The pastor who does not love the work and feel called to it finds ministry overwhelming. On the other hand, greatly blessed are those who so enjoy ministry that their hearts sing in anticipation of returning to the church from vacation.

VIII

LEADERS TAKE RISKS

Since no one gets out alive anyway,
why not do something worthwhile with your life.
    Motto for a Cynical Do-Gooder

After three years of battling what he believed to be a particularly difficult congregation, young Pastor Timothy sought the counsel of older Pastor Paul. "The seminary never taught me how tough things could be in the local church. No matter what I do, it displeases someone. When I helped the youth group sell Christmas trees, the older folks complained that I didn't use the time to visit the elderly. I responded to criticism about my using big words in my sermons by using little words, like *sin*, and then I was accused of getting too personal. One group doesn't like it when I speak about the needs of the poor. 'Too much social action,' they say; 'just preach from the Bible.' If I quote more than seven verses of scripture, another group says I am irrelevant because I don't talk enough about today's issues.

"Things got better for a while. In fact, the last six months have been wonderful. Offerings and attendance have gone up significantly. Unfortunately, things are going so well that the church board decided to remodel the pastor's study and paint the sanctuary. Once again, tension fills my days. I had to raise the money for the project. Now we worship each

Sunday with paint scaffolding in the aisles. During the week the carpenter's noise and dust make it impossible for me to work in my office. "Oh, how I long for quiet and solitude. If only the Lord would lead me into green pastures and make me lie down beside the still waters. What glory there would be if only I could do ministry without taking risks or experiencing tension."

Pastor Paul listened to Timothy. He nodded his graying head in understanding. His brow, pocked by the scars of many church battles, flushed as he responded with what he knew to be an unanticipated commentary. "Timothy, welcome to ministry. Risk, stress, and pain come with the territory. Local church ministry is like taking a moonless midnight stroll through an unmapped mine field. The moments of total bliss are rare. Rather than waste time looking for ways to change or avoid this, learn to make the most of it. With good anticipation and hard work, the risks inherent to the ministry will be transformed into blessings sufficient to make hanging in there worthwhile."

Warning: Life Itself Is Hazardous

Scripture challenges us "therefore . . . choose life" (Deut. 30:19). Regrettably, an affirmative response places us directly in harm's way. Choosing life necessitates risk. We chance having an accident when crossing the street. Sunbathing exposes the body to harmful ultraviolet rays. Making friends leaves us vulnerable to the grief that comes when relationships terminate by decision or death. Marriage makes divorce a possibility. Parenting can become one problem right after another. Choosing life foists risks upon us.

Attempting to live a risk-free existence stifles human possibilities. After all, should we avoid learning to swim lest we become overconfident in the water and drown? Should we avoid learning arithmetic lest we be tempted to cheat on our tax returns? Should we avoid building a dam lest the dam should break?

Graham Chapman never utilized his Oxford University

medical degree. Instead, he became a star on the British comedy show "Monty Python and the Flying Circus." In recent years, he traveled the United States describing his participation in something called the Dangerous Sports Club. This group attracts people who get a thrill from taking risks. Club activities include such events as skiing down sheer mountains in rowboats or wheelchairs, jumping off high bridges tied to long rubber ropes, and being shot from cannons.

Graham Chapman died in late 1989 from a malady totally unrelated to the risks he enjoyed taking. This illness could have afflicted him even if he had agoraphobia and consequently never left the house. A non-biblical proverb holds that wherever there is a good idea, someone will take it too far. Although there are obvious benefits from not taking unnecessary risks, we cannot make life perfectly safe. Even if we removed every danger from the environment, discovered cures for every illness, and so mastered techniques of conflict resolution that we never experienced tension in our relationships, we would still die. We might live 145 years, dry up, and disintegrate into a pile of dust, but we would still die. Life necessitates facing death. Risks can be minimized. They cannot be eliminated.

The Added Risk of Leadership

As he disembarked a plane at the Dallas/Fort Worth airport, a traveler overheard a snippet of conversation between a flight attendant and a man on his way to a Dallas Cowboys football game at Texas Stadium.

"Are you going to make it in time for the game?" the flight attendant inquired.

"Yes, it isn't far from the airport," the man replied.

"I hope it quits raining so you can avoid getting wet," the flight attendant continued.

"It doesn't matter," the man said. "At Texas Stadium, only the players get rained on. The spectators are sheltered from the rain."

Like the Dallas Cowboys, pastors perform their responsibilities in the middle of the field. While those who are center stage frequently receive a little glory, they also get wet first. Assuming a place of leadership adds to the already considerable risks of being human.

By nature of the job, leaders must be willing to get out in front of the crowd where they become visible targets. Anyone harboring a grudge, moving through one of life's difficult transitions, carrying a heavy burden, experiencing unresolved frustration, or feeling angry with God over the inherent unfairness of life feels free to fling a stone at the leader. Experienced clergy persons know that danger comes with the territory. Local church ministry makes the pastor a target for rocks as well as praise. Rather than follow willingly, people tend to tear down those folks who get out in front and try to get the job done. The mantle of leadership should be understood as having a "bull's-eye" painted on it.

Human Beings: The Unpredictable Variables in Every Equation

Compared to ministers, scientists have it easy. They get to work in laboratories, under controlled conditions, with glass beakers and purified chemicals. Well-tested formulas can be applied to their experiments, and outcomes can usually be predicted. Not so when dealing with people—particularly church people. A congregation of only one hundred members represents tens of thousands of unknown and unpredictable variables. What worked extremely well in one situation may have to be altered considerably to work elsewhere. An idea that they loved at Thorntown Church may split the Birdburg church. Ministry is not as predictable as science, nor is the local church as controlled as the laboratory.

Change: Few Find It Fun. Everything and everyone changes. That complicates matters further. Heraclitus noted that we never step twice into exactly the same river. The present always merges with yesterday at the very moment that tomorrow flows naturally into a new today. People change as constantly as the days flow relentlessly onward. But even though people continually change, we can count on people to resist nearly every change. Even when change is slow, almost evolutionary, people seldom like it. Misoneism, the hatred of change, afflicts nearly everyone.

The foolish lament the universality of change and the resistance to it. The wise go beyond tolerating and accepting change to encouraging change and making plans to take advantage of it. They find this more practical than railing about the inevitable. For this reason, pastoral leaders function best by being flexible and responsive to situations. Flexibility, however, should never become aimless wandering. "Let's let things go until we see what happens" does not qualify as an acceptable style of intentional leadership. Flying by the seat of one's britches usually results in arriving at the wrong destination. When left to find their own way, organizations tend to expend their energy, at best, maintaining the status quo or, at worst, drifting toward the dysfunctional. An unpublished corollary of Murphy's Law holds that "all unplanned change tends to be negative and unproductive."

To counter negative drifting, congregations need leaders who lead by acting rather than reacting. Rather than being bound to the past, effective leaders learn how to use the lessons of the past for insight into the present and directions for the future. Doing this puts ministry on the cutting edge. Unfortunately, risks escalate when "what is" and the vision of "what might be" interface. Ministry's choices do not please every person at every moment. Wise leaders make proactive decisions to fulfill their visions of the possible. However, beneficial, well-intentioned, and even morally correct decisions can and will be misunderstood and unappreciated. Consequently, faithful pastors frequently receive negative feedback.

Ministry leads individuals and groups through the gauntlet of self-examination and self-discovery into new possibilities. Walking with people on this frightening journey means that someone will almost always be upset with the pastor. Experienced ministers learn to live with this. They also realize that they cannot irritate people with wreckless abandon. When the local church experiences too much alienation and tension, the pastor loses the authority to lead. Skilled ministers carefully nudge congregations of fragile human beings into growth without pushing them away. This requires a proactive approach to working with people who are regularly unpredictable and sometimes volatile. It also makes being a minister to God's people an incredibly risky business.

Even Religion Adds to the Problem. Naive persons postulate that religion enhances congeniality. They erroneously conclude that working with religious people must be easier than working with the non-religious. Actually, the opposite is true. Scribes and Pharisees, who were considered to be the religious elite, were not only among our Lord's most vocal critics but some of them also schemed with the Romans to have him crucified. History teaches us that there have been as many religious wars as economic wars. In most congregations, those perceived to be the most religious frequently generate the most parish problems and offer the strongest tests for their pastors' skills.

In seeking the counsel of older Pastor Paul, young Pastor Timothy expressed concern about certain members of his congregation. "They drive me nuts," Timothy complained. "One fellow attended a weekend spiritual retreat and now represents himself as a candidate for sainthood. He constantly criticizes me for not preaching 'spiritual' sermons and for not starting sufficient Bible study groups in the congregation. We have another member who writes me letters chastising me for 'theological errors' in my preaching. Still another member constantly harasses me because more of our members do not work at Home Sweet Home Street Mission or the Community Coalition Against Nuclear War. These people are sincere and committed. They live their faith daily, but they push me so hard that my life and ministry are becoming miserable."

"Unfortunately," Pastor Paul responded, "religious fervor can have unpleasant side effects. A fellow minister once observed that we put lightning rods on the church building in memory of the fact that the congregation was once on fire for God. We keep lightning rods in place out of fear that it might happen again.

"Sometimes the flames of religious fervor can be frightening. Rather than being aglow with the presence of God, some people become obnoxious. Fortunately, many, if not most, grow out of this.

"On the other hand, many respond very positively when they hear the Gospel. This can be equally unsettling. The Christian faith can be compared to dynamite. Dynamite has the power to blast a hole in a mine wall or to blow off the hand of the person holding it. Like dynamite, faith can blast open a heart to receive the transforming love of God. Few things can be as exciting as ministering to people who have been transformed by a newly found faith.

"Faith also explodes in ways that make substantial demands on the pastor. That's the risk we take when leading people toward becoming a viable faith community. Preaching puts people in touch with a power that can act as a healing balm or a purifying flame. The same Word that comforts the afflicted will afflict the comfortable. Unfortunately, some people become self-righteous and obnoxious when touched by the Word. Others become angry and recalcitrant. Fortunately, some become infected with a desire to learn more about the faith. Still others develop an insatiable itch to work for peace and justice.

"Of this, though, you can be certain: When the Gospel impacts, things do not remain the same. A congregation on fire with faith makes incredible demands on the pastor. You can count on that."

Failure: One of Ministry's Great Teachers. Driver's education classes use simulators to introduce students to highway hazards. Before putting lives at risk, students sit on benches behind steering wheels and watch videotapes of moving traffic situations. In the safety of a darkened classroom, they practice reacting to approaching stop signs, errant children playing in the street, and pickup trucks making unsignaled lane changes. Although helpful, simulators do not provide the most meaningful driving lessons. Such lessons come when driving an automobile onto a dangerous highway where one can actually experience traffic violations, accidents, and speeding tickets.

Much of the congregational life can also be simulated. Ministers can encourage the people to imagine the perils of living in the wilderness of Sinai or Central America or among the street people of Chicago. We can stimulate loving feelings by talking about a caring fellowship among the members of the church. We can titillate people with talk of the blessedness that comes to those who take seriously the spiritual disciplines of Bible study, prayer, and fasting. These images will be helpful, but they do not equate to living out the faith.

To be the Church that God calls us to be, we must do more than simulate the scenes. We must risk living the scenes. Leadership must do more than activate the mind. It must activate the whole person. Fellowship must be experienced, not merely discussed. Forgiveness must be offered, not merely pondered. The hungry must be fed, not merely lamented. The oppressor must be confronted, not merely cursed. Prayer must be more than a topic for theologizing.

However, when leaders get people "to drive onto the highway," ministry's dangers increase. In addition to the obvious, we risk the probability of frequent failure. Even the most carefully planned programs occasionally fail. Some great ideas never get past the planning stage. The presence of sin in the midst of the human community insures that evil will undermine good. Count on it: Failure happens.

Ministers who fail should count themselves in good company. Abraham, Moses, David, Peter, and the rest of God's leaders know the sting of failure. Apparently, the Creator understands that mere mortals cannot follow the examples of those who do everything successfully.

The badge of failure, like the bull's-eye mentioned previously, comes with the mantle of leadership. Those who wait for the assurance of victory never lead troops into battle. The player who refuses to take her foot off first base until she is absolutely certain that she will make it to second will not set a record for stolen bases. Only those willing to risk defeat or failure open themselves to the possibility of being successful leaders.

Sir Wilfred Grenfell, missionary to Labrador, said it well: "It is courage the world needs, not infallibility." To be an effective pastor, one must function well under prolonged stress, be able to bounce back from regular defeats, and perform ably as an agent of change—while continuing to grow spiritually and remaining optimistic. To do this, a minister needs an above-average supply of courage. Pastors must be graced—for more than the present moment—by the courage that comes with time, courage that makes it possible to survive defeat after defeat and still rejoice about the lessons to be learned from every failure. While this is much to expect, veteran leaders remind us that God's grace is both available and frequently experienced as the courage to keep on keeping on.

Keep This in Mind

A leader of a major denominational organization carried in his wallet a motto attributed to the French Foreign Legion.

"If I falter, push me on.
If I stumble, pick me up.
If I retreat, shoot me."

The call to pastoral leadership should be undertaken with the same resolve. After all, people do not follow programs— even when those programs are needed, are theologically sound, and have the support of the majority. Rather, people follow leaders who inspire them with a vision that steers them in reckless hope for something greater than themselves.

To be effective, pastors must do more than the minimum required. They demand excellence of themselves. They work hard. They take risks. They get out in front and stay there by raising the standards by which they judge themselves and by which they are willing to be judged. While moving challenge to the brink of the terrifying, they help others and themselves to remember that since no one gets out of here alive anyway, we might as well commit ourselves to doing something worthwhile.

---------------------- IX ----------------------

LEADERS LOVE
PEOPLE

*Leadership accepts people where they are
and then takes them somewhere else.*

C. W. Perry

"I feel my ministry at this church has been a total failure," Ben complained to his wife. "Nothing ever happens around here unless I am behind it. When I came to this church, the budget was not fully funded, an average of only one hundred attended worship, and committees very seldom even met. That was six years ago, and nothing has changed. By now we should be seeing results from my work. Instead, we deal with the same problems. I have failed as their minister."

Pastor Ben has a profound misconception about pastoral ministry. He has confused what makes a business executive successful with what makes a pastor effective. While similarities between pastor and corporate executive abound, one significant difference remains. Ministry has no equivalent of profit to report to the stockholders or product to be sold to the public. Instead, ministry specializes in sharing the Gospel with people who might not otherwise hear of God's gift of abundant life. Effectiveness at being a faithful servant of Christ's Church simply cannot be measured as easily as an auto factory counts units sold. Ben rightly strives to be an effective administrator. He has goals of balancing the church budget and making committees function without his continual urging. He goes too far, however, when he assumes that making the congregation function trouble-free constitutes a successful and faithful ministry.

Pastors' experiences can mislead them in regard to the bottom-line objectives of their calling. Ministry cannot be summarized by saying, "I am in the business of oiling ecclesiastical gears and rolling square marbles uphill!" Although pastors experience this kind of work daily, it is not effective ministry. Our central task is to love God's people into wholeness. We have no other product. We are instruments of God's love and Word. God uses us to change the people who can change the world.

For a pastor to function as a leader, he or she must care about people and have a primary commitment to enabling people to grow in their faith. When first called to serve a congregation, the pastor must establish a loving relationship with the people. No matter how important other responsibilities may be, they must wait. In fact, other tasks go much more smoothly when the minister first establishes himself or herself as someone who cares about others. As one older minister recalled, "I conducted funerals for three prominent families during the first two weeks that I was in town. Even though I've never had a more demanding way to start a ministry, it allowed me to quickly establish a bond with those people. They immediately knew that I was a caring pastor. In forty years, I've never had a better ministry."

The minister who does not love people enough to be concerned about their moral and spiritual development not only misses the central meaning of the Christian faith but also fails at leading the congregation. Our Lord understood this need to incorporate love into leadership and made it a requirement for all who would become His followers (John 15:11).[1]

Unfortunately, most of us find love not only difficult to practice but also difficult to understand. We do not always know what it takes to act lovingly as individuals, let alone know how love can be incorporated into leadership. Therefore, another look at Paul's thirteenth chapter of First Corinthians proves helpful. By describing loving and nonloving behavior, this great leader of the early Church both emphasizes the importance of love and clarifies its meaning. Depending on the version of Scripture, translators and paraphrasers list as many as twenty different characteristics of love in I Corinthians 13:1-8.

The Things Love Avoids

Some of Paul's beautiful admonitions are negatively worded. They describe behaviors that should be avoided, primarily because these behaviors serve self at the expense of others. "Love is not jealous or boastful. It is not arrogant or rude. Love does not insist on its own way. It is not irritable or resentful. It does not rejoice at wrong." These admonitions make a good list of diagnostic questions.

Am I Jealous, Boastful, or Proud? A local music club gave an after-recital reception for a noted pianist. Community leaders and ordinary people stood in line with the local newspaper music critic to shake the musician's hand and gush over his performance. As the party wound down, the pianist turned to his hostess and commented, "Well, enough talk about me and what *others* thought of my performance. Let's give *you* a chance to say how much you appreciated me."

Because pulpits, like pianos, occupy places of prominence, preachers, like pianists, deal with the temptations inherent to working center stage. Rather than succumb to pride or jealousy, remember that preaching's accolades come more from having The Story of Life to tell than from one's ability to tell good stories.

Prideful and/or jealous pastors demonstrate more interest in elevating themselves than caring about others. We cannot respect others while being resentful of their accomplishments, nor can we build strength in others when we are wrapped tightly in ourselves. Indeed, love cannot be jealous, boastful, or proud.

Do I Have a Scornful Attitude? This was Pastor Ryan's first trip to the Holy Land. A loud, irritating, "know-it-all" member of the group threatened to ruin the trip for him. At each tour bus stop, she offered running commentary designed to make the group believe that she possessed thorough scriptural knowledge, significant critical thinking skills, and profound theological insight. Pastor Ryan heard enough to realize that she was more buffoon than scholar.

Eventually, an opportunity for Pastor Ryan to put the woman in her place presented itself. The bus stopped at a pile of building stones, which the tour guide described as "the actual ruins of the Inn of the Good Samaritan." The irritating woman was thrilled. "Why, to think we actually stand on the very spot where the Samaritan brought the beaten man. This is the greatest moment of my life," she commented for all to hear.

Pastor Ryan thought about seizing the opportunity. The site was obviously a contrived tourist attraction. The Scripture presents the event as a parable, a story used to illustrate a point. Visiting the "actual Inn of the Good Samaritan" is as critical to faith development as visiting the "actual room where Alice in Wonderland had her tea party" is to understanding the work of Lewis Carroll.

"Why Pastor Ryan, what did you think of that?" she continued to jabber as they returned to the bus.

This was his moment. A few well-chosen comments, given loudly enough for all to hear, would expose the woman as a fool and establish him as the group's most knowledgeable person regarding Holy Land sites.

"I thought it was, well, interesting," Pastor Ryan responded. "Yes, very interesting."

He decided to let the opportunity pass. As sweet as it would have been to cut her down to size, it would not have been a loving thing to do. Paul's description of love includes the admonition to not be scornful of others and not to gloat over their foolishness. Those called to love others cannot pursue selfish advantage—even when others seem to deserve being crushed.

Every congregation has members as irritating as this woman. Pastors continually face the temptation of putting them in their places. Seldom, however, can doing so be justified. Ministers simply cannot make themselves look intelligent by making others look ignorant anymore than they can demonstrate their faithfulness by pointing a finger at the unfaithfulness of others.

Do I Rejoice at the Wrong Others Think They Do? As one pastor explained tongue-in-cheek, "If it wasn't for guilt, I wouldn't be able to motivate this congregation at all. The theme for the soup kitchen Christmas offering is 'Those who have too much should give to those who have so little.' I solicit help for the all-church dinner by pleading that my wife will have to do it if others don't volunteer. 'Make 'em feel guilty,' that's my motto."

While guilt might be appropriately called "the gift that keeps on giving," it fails as an instrument of love. Rather than build, it destroys. Rather than energize, it drains the strength of others. Guilt may be a handy tool, but ministers should not rely on it.

Am I Always Angry? When Pastor Warren resigned Sunday morning, the members of his congregation were dumbfounded. They had known for some time that he had been frustrated. They did not realize, however, just how dissatisfied he had become.

After concluding one of his finest sermons, Pastor Warren stepped to the side of the pulpit, took off his black robe, placed it over the back of a nearby chair, and announced, "I shall never wear that symbol of office again. As of this morning, I resign as minister of this congregation. I am also leaving the ministry of the Church of Jesus Christ.

"I just cannot take it any longer. I have wearied of holding the banner for peace in a world gone mad promoting war. I am angry that society remains blind to the needs of the poor and oppressed. I am also angry with this congregation. You have never given me the support I have needed in the struggle for peace and justice."

Pastor Warren permitted anger to derail his ministry. It can happen easily. During the past generation, mainline churches have been on the forefront of significant social issues. Church leaders have been deeply involved in everything from the struggle for civil rights to protesting the war in Vietnam to confronting issues of injustice in South Africa and Central America. There has been and there remains an enormous amount of evil in this world, and mainline churches have spent an enormous amount of time and energy being angry at the world's evil. Our pulpits ring with righteous indignation. Our denominational headquarters regularly, justly, and dutifully express their displeasure. Our national assemblies offer carefully prepared and well-reasoned corrective solutions to global problems. Like many local church pastors, Warren rages continually at racism, sexism, militarism, individualism, and every other unjust, oppressive "ism."

While one can understand and even support this reaction, pastoral ministers simply cannot permit themselves to harbor excessive anger. Even when anger can be explained as "righteous indignation," those consumed by rage undermine the ministry of the church. Pastors who rail excessively against the evil in this world do not do their most faith-filled work. Mere mortals simply cannot generate sufficient energy to share the Good News while expressing continual rage. Those who try wear themselves out.

The Ephesian dictum directs those who seek to be faithful to "be angry but sin not." Although this is never easy, effective leaders develop ways to express anger nondestructively. They learn to remain indignant at the sin of the world while remaining sensitive to the needs of the sinners.

Do I Hold Grudges? Pastors must cultivate an inordinate capacity for forgiveness. Local church ministry offers little space for holding grudges. Congregations are never large enough to permit "writing-off" the irritating, the irascible, the troubled, or those with whom the pastor has had differences. Our faith teaches that the price has already been paid for human sin. Forgiveness is free for the asking. The minister who does not model this truth in his or her relationships cannot preach it convincingly to others.

To love, one cannot hold a grudge, rely on guilt, or vent anger with reckless abandon. What a tough assignment this is for those who are committed to loving people but who continue to hate evil and injustice, who believe guilt is a handy motivational tool, and who have convinced themselves that a quick temper should be worn as a badge of honor. Paul, however, insists that these unloving behaviors can and must be extinguished from the actions of the faithful.

For some, this will require taking lessons in how to motivate without resorting to guilt. For others, considerable willpower will have to be applied to achieve a "be angry but sin not" reaction pattern. For the persistently unforgiving, professional counseling may be needed. Fortunately, however, faith does not leave us to our own devices. Since love is a matter of grace, the capacity to act lovingly can come as a gift from a caring God.

The Things Love Seeks to Do

Love expects more than the avoidance of negative behaviors. Love requires that positive actions be done in the best interests of others. As Paul wrote, "Love is patient and kind. It rejoices in the right. Love bears all things, believes all things, hopes all things, endures all things. Love never ends" (I Cor. 13:4a, 6b, 7, 8a).

Do I Look for Ways to Be Constructive? The business axiom holds, "Produce what the public wants and sell it for a profit." While this is a tempting premise for a congregation, the Church of Jesus Christ cannot be built on this principle. We are called, after all, to be faithful. The road of faithfulness does not always lead to worldly success.

Rather than focus on what people think they *want*, the Church must focus on what people really *need*. The differences can be profound. Rich folks' itch for more money usually can be satisfyingly scratched with experiences in the blessedness of giving. People might want to be excused for their racism when they need to be confronted with it. Some folks want their sinful life-styles to be blessed when they need to be converted. Those who lack a strong sense of self-worth may benefit the most from the assurance that God loves and accepts them in the midst of their human frailties—even when they think that they want something else.

The pastoral leader frequently demonstrates caring for members of the congregation by distinguishing what they want from what they really need. This constitutes the hard edge of loving. The kindness of which Paul speaks in I Corinthians 13:4 does not always mean doing what pleases people at the present moment. Loving actions must be constructive. The capacity to discern what people really need is grace-given and anticipates an intimate knowledge of people and requires putting others' health and well-being before personal needs or popularity.

As Paul suggests, "loving as kindness" comes in a package tied with a long string of patience. The dictionary defines *patience* as "enduring pain and trouble with composure and without complaining." By definition, this kind of love tolerates insult, delay, and confusion. Every pastor is intimately acquainted with the need for patience. Occasions of frustration, trouble, insult, and failure abound. Ministers motivated to distinguish between what people think they want and what people really need have had at least an occasional day when they have thought, "Compared to me, Job had it easy!"

Do I Believe the Best About People? The seminary professor told of one of his regular practices to a graduating class, "At least one night each week, before I leave for home, I walk down the hall where the class photos hang. I stop before a different class each week and look over the photos. I think about the individual members of that class and remember each as a special student. I like to focus on the gifts of every person in the class. Then I pray for each class member in his or her current place of ministry. Particularly, I pray that all will realize their full potential as God's servants."

Every pastoral minister's relationship with the congregation can benefit from the lesson taught by this seminary professor. Leadership and love interface when the art of seeing people as having great potential is a constant practice. Loving decisions are not based on what enhances one's career. A pastor's goal must be more than producing a larger congregation with a bigger budget. Ministers must be concerned with putting people in touch with the power of faith.

Helping others grow spiritually requires a willingness to listen—long and sincerely. Love cannot be too busy for people. It takes an abundance of time and careful listening to develop relationships that open the channels through which others see their own potential. Arranging for the secretary to interrupt an undesirable or inconvenient meeting by announcing a staged "emergency" is not love. Ministry accepts people for themselves and then strives to lead them to realize their fullest potentials for service to God and others. Love always has the best interest of others at heart.

Do I Endure Whatever Is Hurled at Me? Pastors soon learn that much will be hurled at them. Leaders frequently see things before others do. They are guided by a vision, which may or may not always be clear to others. They lead by reason enhanced by intuition. This results in frequent misunderstanding and criticism. Consequently, much will be hurled at the leader. Those who strive to love, however, do not give up. As Paul writes, "Love never fails." It keeps on keeping on!

Leadership Insights from I Corinthians 13:1-8
(A paraphrase that takes great liberties.)
 If I preach such an eloquent, prophetic sermon that the church softball team misses a game to work at an inner-city soup kitchen, yet I rejoice more in the publicity received than

the hungry fed, I have not acted lovingly. Consequently, I have not been faithful to my call to ministry.

If an adult Sunday school class I teach grows so large that we must meet in the sanctuary, yet I plan my lessons more to elicit strokes for my ego than to offer challenges from the Scripture, I present myself instead of Christ and am not a loving pastor.

If I work seven days each week, balance the church budget, build a family life center, maintain a 15 percent new member addition rate year after year, and even burn out in the process, yet people neither hear about nor experience being the valued children of a loving God, my ministry cannot be acclaimed as successful.

Those called to lead the Church must love the people. To be a loving pastor, one must be genuinely concerned for the spiritual health and well-being of others. To value others, certain positive behaviors must be actively pursued, while negative, destructive actions are scrupulously avoided. Stated most briefly, love means doing those things that are in the best interests of others instead of doing what serves self best.

X

LEADERS VALUE ADMINISTRATION

All managers need not be leaders,
but all leaders must know how to manage.

Don Conant

Do not equate pastoral leadership with administration. Ministers who lead do much more than organize to get things done. Note this, however: To lead effectively, one must be a competent manager. The ability to manage enables and empowers the other tasks of leadership.

Pastors who lack administrative skills can be easily identified. Their ministries fall into predictable, frequently repetitive patterns. For eighteen months to two years after a pastor arrives to serve a congregation, everything goes smoothly. For those who are gifted preachers or have charismatic personalities, this time is typically characterized by a flourish of congregational growth. Worship attendance increases significantly. New members join regularly. The laity are overheard telling their friends about "our wonderful new minister" and how "our church is healthier than it has been in years."

Then problems begin to arise. Many of the new members stop coming to worship. They have never felt included in the membership. New groups were never started to assimilate them beyond morning worship. Before long, the rest of the congregation begins to drift into old habits. Instead of attending weekly, some return to their once-a-month worship attendance. Others simply stay home Sunday morning and read the newspaper. Two years after the best worship attendance average in twenty years, the congregation has shrunk back to the same size it was before the present minister came.

Key lay leaders begin to grumble. "He does not return my phone calls." "She did not follow through on the task that she promised to complete for the church cabinet." "Instead of delegating, he tries to do everything himself." "She has great ideas and always seems busy, but she never accomplishes anything!"

Typically—no later than the fourth year—the minister shows symptoms of burnout. Often, such clergy persons evaluate their circumstances by saying something like, "I had two great years before things began to deteriorate. I am not certain why that happened. The church may have had some deep-seated problems of which I was unaware. Maybe there is something wrong with me. Perhaps, I have an insufficient faith commitment. I only know that the new members stopped coming and the old members lost confidence in me."

Rather than being symptomatic of a troubled congregation or a dysfunctional pastor, this pattern can usually be explained as poor church administration. The minister did not know how to get things done. Congregations that flourish know how to plan, set realistic goals, and organize to reach those goals through faith and action. Almost always, this means that the pastors know and practice good administrative skills. As Paul mandates, "They do things decently and in order" (I Cor. 14:40).

Of course, good management techniques do not, in and of themselves, build dynamic faith communities. An effective minister does more than handle daily chores adequately. However, when day to day routines are left unattended, the congregation deteriorates.

Distinguishing Leadership Skills from Administrative Skills

After taking a seminar, a minister was overheard saying, "There are two simple differences between a leader and a manager. To begin with, you manage work and lead people. Human beings are not tools, tasks, or inventory. Consequently, you cannot 'manage' people. You must lead people. Secondly, administrative types content themselves by maintaining the status quo. They keep the train on the tracks and on schedule. Leaders, on the other hand, dream up new routes and schedules for the railroad. They seek to change 'what is' to 'what might be.' Come to think of it, that explains why managers and leaders disagree so much of the time."

Although oversimplified, these points are well-taken. Writers on this topic make similar distinctions between those who function primarily as leaders and those who function primarily as managers. John Gardner contends that these two groups do not think or act alike.[1] Administrators, he suggests, appeal to logic, work through existing structures, and make decisions based on established goals. Leaders, on the other hand, permit vision and intuition to inform their logic—something a pure manager seldom does. Leaders also tend to value existing decision-making structures only to the extent that those structures facilitate the empowerment of the vision that the leader pursues. For leaders, the vision assumes a higher priority than the decision-making structures. Geoffrey Bellman suggests that these groups do not treat resources in the same way. Administrators manage resources. That, Bellman points out, is the logical extension of their desire to maintain the status quo. Leaders, on the other hand, set expanding resources as their goal.[2]

Scripture distinguishes leadership from administration more simply. Both are called spiritual gifts. Leadership, as described in Romans 8:12, I Thessalonians 5:12, I Timothy 3:4 and 5:17, means to direct or govern others, often for their protection. Administration is mentioned only in Romans 12:8. The Greek word used here means "one who guides toward a goal." As an example, it identifies the pilot responsible for bringing ships into harbor.

Biblically speaking, administrators can thus be distinguished from leaders by the functions that each performs. The leader sets the goals and exercises care for the group. The administrator accepts the goals set by others and executes the plans to accomplish them.[3] As with all gifts of God, leadership and administration can be enhanced by training, experience, and commitment.

Even a "People Person" Must Manage

Lyle and Andy were discussing their relative strengths and weaknesses as ministers. "The way I see it," Lyle started, "I am a 'people person.' In fact, I care so much about the needs of people that I sometimes neglect administrative duties. I have learned to live with that, however. God did not call me to attend meetings, formulate plans, and complete forms for the bishop's office. Fortunately, my pastoral heart overrides the guilt I experience when I don't get things done 'decently and in good order.'

"Unfortunately, I have a great deal of guilt to overcome. I don't spend the necessary time to prepare meaningful sermons, support committees, or develop a long-range plan and the strategy to implement it. I spend most of my time visiting shut-ins, calling on families, or just sitting around Johnson's Cozy Corner Cafe talking to anyone who drops in. Frankly, the church shows the results of my inattentiveness to detail. I love the people and they love me, but not much really happens at the church I serve."

"I could use some of your love for people," Andy responded. "I am too task-oriented. Sometimes, I think God called me to run the office rather than to serve in the office of ministry. Meeting, planning, studying, and reporting take most of my time. I seldom find time to visit those in the hospital, let alone to make routine home visits. Our committees operate smoothly, but I don't even know the congregation very well. In fact, I sometimes wonder if I manage a business or pastor a church."

Andy and Lyle analyze another dimension of the administrative-leadership issue. Their discussion demonstrates that pastors cannot choose between being task-oriented managers and people-loving leaders. An effective ministry requires both. One must love people and be sufficiently organized to get the job done.

The totally task-oriented manager sees people as tools rather than as children of God. Such a person might be tempted to fill out an accident form before calling an ambulance. Obviously, pastoral ministry cannot tolerate callousness to human need.

On the other hand, having concern for people to the neglect of management does not work either. An absolutely people-centered minister might cancel the stewardship drive in favor of an all-church party. In business, supervisors who are more concerned for people than for the accomplishment of tasks are called "country club managers." Their employees take work breaks instead of coffee breaks. Congregations enjoy a pastor like this until the church begins to suffer institutional neglect.

Scripture describes a leader as both a caring person and an able manager. Certainly our Lord modeled total concern for people while running an "organization." He recruited twelve associates to assist with his ministry and then organized them for action. Even officers were chosen. Judas served as treasurer, and Peter was appointed post-Passion week leader. While performing administrative duties, Jesus never neglected the needs of people or his own spiritual needs.

After the Resurrection, a group of leaders remained who had learned their lessons well. As the church expanded, demands on the apostles to run the organization and to care for the needs of people escalated. The early church desperately needed both attentive management and inspirational leadership. The apostles responded quickly and appropriately. Deacons were appointed to handle day-to-day operations. A policy council met to make decisions and to keep lines of communication open. Missionaries were appointed to continue spreading the Good News. These and other well-recognized management techniques empowered the apostles to lead the church without neglecting the needs of the people or the organization.

Four Indispensable Principles of Church Management

This chapter is intended only to remind the reader that leaders must also manage. It does not attempt even to outline the principles of church administration. There are four skills, however, that pastors must learn and practice to be effective managers.

1. Build a Cadre of Capable and Committed Helpers. Joyce had never chaired the nominating committee. Because she wanted to do the right thing the right way, she called Pastor Lucy to announce the time and place of the first meeting. "Now, I know you are busy and might not have time for this," Joyce cheerfully said to Pastor Lucy, "but I want you to know that you are certainly welcome to come if you want."

Pastor Lucy, a local church leader with twenty years of experience and a reputation for both inspirational leadership and competent management, said, "I promise you, Joyce, I will be there. In fact, I will come to every meeting of the nominating committee. I have a personal policy never to miss giving input when lay leaders are chosen."

Much of Lucy's positive leadership reputation results from taking seriously the selective recruitment and careful training of the laity. She steers clear of surrounding herself with friends or those whose support of the pastor constitute their only qualification for office. Instead, she encourages the selection of who can do the job. She understands that the health of a congregation rises and falls on the quality, commitment, and skills of the people who accept and complete responsibilities.

Our Lord followed a similar pattern. When he needed help, he recruited apostles, not necessarily based on their support for him but on their ability to get things done. As

Lucy states the principle, "Recruit eagles and teach them to fly. That advances the Lord's work and keeps the pastor's life happy at the same time."

2. Delegate Work to That Cadre of Committed and Capable Helpers. It makes no sense to recruit and train good help and then not to give them anything to do. Yet, many pastors do just that. They retain every activity as their personal responsibility. Some do not even delegate the most routine tasks, such as sorting mail, typing letters, paying bills, ordering supplies, unlocking the building on Sunday morning, or mowing the lawn. If Jesus had behaved similarly, then he himself would have gone for the donkey that he rode into Jerusalem (Mark 11:1-3). In fact, he might never have called apostles in the first place.

Carl George and Robert Logan offer a simple way to determine what can be delegated. It can be summarized by the following steps:

a. List all current activities.
b. Eliminate unnecessary activities.
c. Circle the tasks others can do.
d. Put an asterisk by each one that only the minister can do.
e. Delegate to others everything without an asterisk.

If more than a few activities have asterisks, the pastor has an inflated notion of self-importance. Go back, and do the exercise again.

George and Logan continue by offering criteria for what others should not be asked to do. Do not delegate the following:

a. *Responsibility to correct or discipline.* For instance, if the church secretary takes two hours for lunch rather than the agreed upon one-half hour, the minister must talk to him or her about it. "It's personally unpleasant" does not constitute a sufficient reason to delegate a responsibility.
b. *Tasks that involve confidential information.* If a question

arises about whether or not something should be public, do not delegate it. Mishandling anything confidential can destroy a pastor's credibility.

c. *Responsibility to create and maintain morale.* The minister remains responsible for the spiritual and emotional climate of the congregation.[4]

Learn to delegate and do it regularly. Clergy persons who don't delegate hurt themselves and the church.

3. Stay Attentive to the Details. The leader's responsibility does not end with delegating. As A. T. Cushman, CEO of Sears, explains, "The art of administration is constant checking."[5]

Our Lord adhered to this principle. He delegated work by sending out the seventy-two (Luke 10). He did not, however, merely turn over the responsibility of proclaiming the Good News to others. He carefully selected, trained, and supported them. When they returned, he evaluated their work. Jesus practiced the twin arts of delegating and constant checking.

4. Manage Time Well and Carefully. Most ministers yearn for time management insights. For this reason, dozens of books have been written on the topic. The following is simply a list of ten principles of time management for clergy.

a. *God gives us time as a gift.* Everything else is secondary to this principle. We must be faithful stewards of God's priceless gift of time.

b. *Each person has the same amount of time available each day.* No one has more or less than 86,400 seconds per day.

c. *You can take charge of your time.* In fact, if you don't make decisions on how to use your time, others will.

d. *Be clear about your objectives.* Be ready to give succinct answers to questions such as: What drives you in ministry? What are you trying to accomplish? How does what God calls you to do compare with what others expect you to do? Those with a clear understanding of these issues are less likely to become sidetracked by trivial activities.

e. *Establish your priorities on the basis of your objectives.*

Everything worthwhile does not relate to your objectives, and all of your objectives are not of equal value. One cannot be equally devoted to 101 tasks—even when all are worthy. A minister only has so much energy to offer. Those who try to do all things at all times exhaust themselves quickly.

Effective congregations constantly evaluate mission and ministry. Less effective congregations patch their program together, using the favorite activities introduced by former ministers. Frequently, this means continuing to do things that no longer work well. Knowing your priorities permits the elimination of irrelevant and unproductive activities.

f. *Plan for interruptions.* Be certain, however, not to be controlled by them. If the minister is not careful, his or her day can become a series of interruptions interrupted by interruptions. Herb Miller suggests the following priorities for letting things interrupt you: (a) God, for example, Bible study and prayer, (b) spouse, (c) children, (d) church leaders, (e) church members, (f) non-members, (g) denominational work, (h) civic work.[6]

g. *Break big jobs into small parts.* This keeps one from being discouraged by the enormity of the task. Jesus did it that way. When faced with the task of feeding the 5,000, the apostles wanted to send everyone home. The job overwhelmed them. Jesus, on the other hand, broke the big job into little parts. He had the people sit in small groups, he inventoried the fish and bread available, prayed fervently, and then he got started feeding the people. Big, impossible jobs can usually be broken into smaller, possible components.

h. *Plan ahead.* Many projects fail because of insufficient lead time. Put projects on the calendar far in advance. Avoid waiting until the last minute to complete details. Plan your time in weeks and months, not in hours and minutes.

i. *Resolve to become a better manager of your time.* Buy and study a good book on the topic of time management. Talk to experienced ministers who get things done efficiently and maintain their sanity.

j. *Do it now!* It will not be any easier or take any less time if you procrastinate.

A Final Word

A story is told of a lighthouse along a bleak coast. Only enough oil to keep the lamp in the lighthouse burning nightly was delivered each month. A woman asked the lighthouse keeper for oil to keep her children warm. In spite of the short supply, the keeper took pity on her and granted her request. Then a farmer came. His son needed oil for a lamp so that he could study at night. Still another needed oil for an engine. The keeper cared deeply for each of those people and granted their requests.

Near the end of the month, the oil tank in the lighthouse ran dry. The beacon could not be lighted. That night three ships crashed on the rocks. More than one hundred lives were lost. The lighthouse keeper helped a few people and, in the process, lost the lives of many.

Without the organizational skills and discipline required for competent management, our attempts to love others can degenerate into warm feelings and random flourishes of well-intentioned but not necessarily helpful actions. Pastoral leaders must know how to manage.

NOTES

Introduction

1. James MacGregor Burns, *Leadership* (New York: Harper and Row, 1978), p. 4.

1. Leaders Lead People

1. "When There Are Reins, Loyalty Won't Reign," *PMA Advisor* (April 1987): 5.
2. Paul L. Brown, *Managing Behavior on the Job* (New York: John Wiley and Sons, 1982), p. 6.
3. Herb Miller, *How to Build a Magnetic Church* (Nashville: Abingdon Press, 1987), p. 116.
4. These are called the basic tasks of ministry. John C. Harris, *Stress, Power and Ministry* (Washington, D.C.: The Alban Institute, 1977), p. 23.
5. Geoffrey Bellman, *The Quest for Staff Leadership* (Glenview, Ill.: Scott, Foresman and Company, 1986), p. 16.

2. Leaders Gather People Around a Vision

1. *The Executive Speechwriter Newsletter* 3, No. 5: 2.
2. Clovis G. Chappel, *Sermons from the Parables* (Nashville: Abingdon Press, 1979), pp. 65-66.
3. David Rockefeller, as quoted by Gary Inrig, "Between Trapezes! Involvement and Delegation," *Interest* (April 1987): 4.

4. "Move Only Forward," *Our Daily Bread* 32, nos. 6, 7, 8 (September 5, 1987): 17.

3. Leaders Motivate People

1. Lyle Schaller, *Getting Things Done* (Nashville: Abingdon Press, 1986), p. 123.
2. Clement Stone, *PMA Adviser* 6, no. 6 (June 1987): 1.
3. C. Kirk Hadaway, "Growing Off the Plateau: A Summary of the 1988 'Church on the Plateau' Survey" (Nashville: Sunday School Board of the Southern Baptist Convention, 1989).

4. Leaders Encourage People

1. Roger Herman, *The Process of Excelling* (Cleveland: Oakhill Press, 1988), p. 71.
2. Southern Baptist Church Study on Plateau Churches.
3. Fred Smith, "The Minister As Maestro," *Leadership* (Fall 1988): 130-37.
4. David Keirsey and Marilyn Bates, *Please Understand Me: Character and Temperament Types* (Del Mar, Calif.: Prometheus Nemesis Book Company, 1984), p. 129.
5. *Discovering Your Gifts* (Grand Rapids: Christian Reformed Home Missions, 1983), pp. 56-57.
6. Robert Greenleaf, *The Servant As Leader* (Cambridge: Center for Applied Studies, 1970), pp. 13-14.
7. James Burke, *What Works For Me: Interviews With 16 Chief Executives* (New York: Random House, 1986).
8. *The Executive Speechwriter Newsletter* 3, no. 3: 2.
9. Richard Jessen, "Preaching on the Lessons" *Church Management: The Clergy Journal* (October 1987): 19.

5. Leaders Are Role Models

1. Thomas Oden, *Pastoral Theology: Essentials of Ministry* (San Francisco: Harper & Row, 1983), p. 68.
2. Roger Herman, *The Process of Excelling*, p. 36.
3. Goodrich & Sherwood Company, New York, reported in *Business Bulletins*, undated.

NOTES

4. Raymond J. Bakke and Samuel K. Roberts, *The Expanded Mission of 'Old First' Churches* (Valley Forge: Judson Press, 1986), pp. 99-103.

6. Leaders Expect Excellence

1. Gordan MacDonald, *Ordering Your Private World* (Chicago: Moody Press, 1984), pp. 94-95.
2. Roger Herman, *The Process of Excelling*, p. 28.
3. Barry McMurtrie, *Time Out* (Berwick, Victoria, Australia: Vital Publications, 1980), p. 28.
4. *Leadership Magazine* 7, no. 1 (Winter 1986): 40.
5. Lyle Schaller, *The Change Agent* (Nashville: Abingdon Press, 1972), p. 54.
6. Herb Miller and Doug Moore, *300 Seed Thoughts* (Lubbock, Tex.: Net Press, 1986), p. 139.

7. Leaders Work Hard

1. Tex Sample, *Blue-Collar Ministry* (Valley Forge: Judson Press, 1984), p. 25.
2. James D. Glasse, *Putting It Together in the Parish* (Nashville: Abingdon Press, 1972), pp. 55-56.

9. Leaders Love People

1. Myron Bush, *The New Leader* (Wheaton, Ill.: Victor Books, 1987), p. 89.

10. Leaders Value Administration

1. John Gardner, as quoted by David Broder, "Good Manager Bush Is Still Not a Leader," *Fort Worth Star-Telegram*, November 29, 1989, sec. 1.
2. Goeffrey Bellman, *The Quest for Staff Leadership* (Glenview, Ill.: Scott, Foresman and Company, 1986), pp. 15, 16.
3. *Discover Your Gifts* (Grand Rapids: Christian Reformed Home Missions, 1983), pp. 50, 68.

THE VITAL CHURCH LEADER

4. Carl George and Robert Logan, *Leading and Managing Your Church* (Old Tappan, N.J.: Fleming H. Revell and Company, 1987), p. 118.

5. Fred Smith, *Learning to Lead* (Copublished by Christianity Today and Word, Inc., 1986), p. 39.

6. Herb Miller, "Time Management for Ministers," audiotape available from National Evangelism Association, Lubbock, Tex.